TEXAS
HILL COUNTRY
CUISINE

★ FLAVORS FROM THE ★

CABERNET GRILL
TEXAS WINE COUNTRY RESTAURANT

Chef Ross Burtwell
with Julia Celeste Rosenfeld

PHOTOGRAPHY BY JENNIFER WHITNEY

Creative Noggin Press | P.O. Box 460109, San Antonio, Texas 78246 | www.creativenoggin.com

ISBN-13: 978-0-9899450-0-4
Library of Congress Catalog Number: 2013952379

All photos by Jennifer Whitney, except for photos on pages 2, 4–6, 12, 14, 16, 18, 21–22, 26, 56, 78, 79, 92, 154, 175 and back cover by Steve Rawls

First Edition | Printed In Canada

Dedication

This book is dedicated, first, to all of the people who had an impact on my early culinary career: The teachers, trainers and explorers who helped me learn the finer points of all things culinary as I developed the craft I love. You planted the seeds that have allowed me to grow. The list starts with Mark, the first guy I stepped on the cooks' line with at 4:30 in the morning some 25 years ago, and who taught me how to flip an egg, and then Hans, Steve, Woerner, Jim, Beth, Sherri, Tong, James, Dave, Timm and Ken-Bob. I will forever be in debt to each of you.

To my parents, who provided me with a great upbringing, teaching me to be respectful, kind and caring to those around me: Thanks to my mom for instilling me with a sense of what good, wholesome food is all about, and my father for teaching me to push a bit further than those around me so I could achieve higher results. I appreciate your love and support throughout the years.

To my entire staff of the Cabernet Grill and the Cotton Gin Village: Your hard work and the dedication that you show on a daily basis provides a wonderful experience for the guests who visit our establishment. Your commitment to being professional, friendly and continually quality-minded makes my job so much easier and pleasurable. I know you've got my back, and I thank you.

But most of all, this book is dedicated to my family: Mariana, Marissa and Hunter. I love you each to no end. You make my life complete.

★ ★ ★ ★ ★

FOREWORD

Terry Thompson-Anderson, CCP
Executive Chef and Author of
The Texas Hill Country: A Food and Wine Lover's Paradise
and *Texas on the Plate*

FREDERICKSBURG, TEXAS

I have known and admired Ross Burtwell for many years—as both a personal friend and a fellow chef and professional colleague. We have worked together on culinary-based community projects in our town of Fredericksburg many times, and I can confidently say that he is an amazing man. Ross came to Fredericksburg to manage the kitchen of a restaurant and bed and breakfast property here that was for sale, harboring the dream of owning his own restaurant. The place was called the Cotton Gin Seafood & Steak Kitchen. The kitchen's main focus was on Cajun food, so he got a good background in that popular cuisine while heading up the kitchen. Ross was intrigued by the possibilities that the place set dancing in his head. After carefully arranging his financing, he purchased the property the following year and set about to turn his vision of establishing his own signature restaurant into reality.

When he took over, Ross renamed the grounds the Cotton Gin Restaurant & Lodging. From his first day of ownership, he began the arduous process of finding his culinary niche in the Texas Hill Country. He created an inviting ambiance around a one-of-a-kind setting best described as "rustic elegance." It's cozy and casual, but the tables are impeccably set—suitable for diners dressed in tourist wear or evening fare.

Ross brought his considerable talents as a chef and a superior head for business to the table. Having a very instinctive feel for the type of food that was becoming known as "Hill Country Cuisine," a blend of locally raised, grass-fed meats and produce, field-harvested Texas game meats and birds, local cheeses and condiments—all kissed by our unique Hill Country terroir—Ross began to build his menu, and his reputation, on his vision of sourcing his ingredients

9

★ ★ ★ ★ ★

locally. Seafood has been sourced from the bounty of our Texas coastal waters from the beginning. He signed up with the Texas Department of Agriculture's GO TEXAN Restaurant program and quickly became known as a staunch advocate of Texas agriculture. It all worked, and word of the kitchen's excellence began to spread far beyond Fredericksburg.

Then, in 2007, after watching the Texas wine industry consistently raise its bar of excellence, Ross made the decision to "bet the farm" on establishing an all-Texas label wine list. He wasn't sure what to expect, but he knew that his Texas-inspired dishes, with ingredients sourced from Texas, were a perfect match to Texas-grown and produced wines. Within a few short months, wine sales at the restaurant had doubled. As he began to select varietals from various Texas

wineries, he'd load up his entire serving staff and take them to the wineries for private tastings and education from the winemakers, or the winemakers would come to the restaurant to teach the staff about their respective wines. Ross makes sure that the wait staff can suggest wine pairings with each menu item and answer diners' questions about the wines with confidence. He changes the offerings often, rotating new varietals, or new wineries, onto the wine list. He renamed the restaurant the Cabernet Grill Texas Wine Country Restaurant and renamed the cottages the Cotton Gin Village.

As a chef, I recognize the results of Ross's dedication to the craft. I established a reputation for excellence in the food I created, and demanded high standards from the staff at my own restaurant on the "Redneck Riviera"

★ ★ ★ ★ ★

★ ★ ★ ★ ★

of the Mississippi Gulf Coast. I can whip up some fine grub in my home kitchen too, but, like many chefs, I enjoy eating out and having someone else serve me on occasion. However, I am often a tough critic. When I dine out, I expect to be wowed by the entire experience—the food, the appropriateness of the wine list, the service, the ambiance. I choose to patronize the restaurants of chefs who are as meticulous with the details and the quality of food as I have always been. Over my years of dining at the Cabernet Grill, Ross has never disappointed my expectations. Each time I leave sated from yet another fine dining experience. And I look forward to the next time I return for some gustatory pampering.

This is a very impressive book from which I am sure you will enjoy cooking. The recipes are clear, concise, and easy to follow, and the Texas-centric ingredients are readily available. Having worked with Ross on some of his recipes for my own books, I know that he possesses a trait that not many chefs have—the knowledge of how to construct a good recipe. The range of dishes in this book reflects the diversity of the menu at the Cabernet Grill—from luscious simple dishes to more succulent, complex undertakings. Ross is not afraid to "give away his secrets" as are many chefs. They're here for the learning, to make sure that your efforts at recreating his dishes in your kitchen are successful—and delicious! I know that I personally can't wait to get into my own kitchen with the book to duplicate some of the menu items I've enjoyed so often at the Cabernet Grill, but couldn't quite nail the ingredients in my mind's tongue!

★ ★ ★ ★ ★

Contents

* * * * *

* * * * *

DEFINING TEXAS HILL COUNTRY CUISINE

When we began researching and preparing for this book, we realized there isn't another cookbook that identifies itself and follows through as presenting Texas Hill Country Cuisine. Yes, it is a cuisine unto itself, and we feel the dishes we serve at the Cabernet Grill are among the quintessential flavors that define it. ★ What are the hallmarks of Texas Hill Country Cuisine? It is food created by people who understand the importance of combining area-specific, locally grown and produced ingredients—seasonally sourced—and matching it with Texas-grown grapes and locally produced wines. Texas Hill Country Cuisine is the ultimate dining synergy for food and wine lovers. ★ This cookbook is a guide to understanding the unique tastes and aromas of Texas Hill Country cuisine, and a celebration of the marriage of those flavors with Texas wines. ★ The recipes range from simple to complex. We've included classics you can find on the menu at the Cabernet Grill and others created just for special wine dinners. If you've eaten a dish in my restaurant and loved it, this book will help you recreate it at home. If you wish you had ordered it but didn't, now you can make it anytime. And when you decide to serve a special wine dinner at home, this will serve as your idea book.

★★★★★

ABOUT THE COTTON GIN VILLAGE AND THE CABERNET GRILL

The Cotton Gin Village is a set of seven unique, rustic 19th century log cabins just outside the main shopping area of Fredericksburg, Texas. Nestled around a courtyard filled with native plants, bubbling koi pond and serene waterfalls, it evokes the ambiance of a small 1870s Hill Country village, complete with wagons, a tank house and an old cotton gin. It's the perfect home base for explorers who want to venture into all that the area offers: wineries, orchards, walking trails, horseback riding, charming shops and antiques.

Guests often sit for hours on their front porch rockers simply enjoying the birds, butterflies and clean air. Each cabin is a small home with a living area and cozy wood fireplace, mini kitchen, bedroom and bathroom—complete with a Jacuzzi tub—and each is tastefully decorated with antiques and rustic décor. Yes, there are also the modern conveniences of air conditioning, heat, satellite TV and a wireless network.

Unlike a traditional bed and breakfast, we provide our guests with breakfast in the privacy of their cabins, so no one has to dress for breakfast and chat at a table of strangers. We stock every cabin with a selection of coffee and tea, freshly baked pastries, juice and milk. You'll also be treated to several servings of the Cotton Gin Village House-Made Granola—enough for breakfast and snacks.

LEAVE GUNS HERE

Bring your whole gang of up to 12 to 1 Big House at the Cotton Gin Village for a rustically modern Hill Country retreat.

My wife Mariana and I have owned and managed the Cotton Gin Village since 2003, and I've been the executive chef at our on-site restaurant, the Cabernet Grill, since 2001. We have built a strong reputation for our dining menu, as well as our 100% Texas wine list.

In the summer of 2008, the Cabernet Grill was ranked the top restaurant in the nation by TripAdvisor.com, and it has remained among the site's top-ranked restaurants ever since. I credit our entire team for that ongoing honor. In 2012, OpenTable listed us as one of the top 100 American restaurants in the nation, among notables such as The French Laundry, Per Se, Fearing's and Craft.

NOW ABOUT OUR TEAM ———————

Mariana and I met in a professional kitchen in 1991. She was the most sought-after prep chef in San Antonio and I was the newly hired sous chef at Cascabel restaurant in the Sheraton Fiesta. Mariana was legendary for her speed, precision and great attitude. Now by my side for more than 20 years, in and out of the kitchen, she can still outwork anyone. I credit her for instilling that strong work ethic in our two children, Marissa and Hunter, who often pitch in to help with tasks at the Cotton Gin Village and the Cabernet Grill. We are also fortunate to have an extremely hardworking culinary staff in the kitchen and an exceptional management and service staff in the dining area. I attribute much of our success to this outstanding group of individuals.

Mariana Burtwell

FROM TEXAS, BY TEXANS

My biggest source of pride is in the partnerships the Cabernet Grill has forged with local farmers, vintners and entrepreneurs. This allows us to present our guests with outstanding Texas food and wine. I gravitated to these honest ingredients since my early days as a chef in Dallas, just as the Southwestern Cuisine movement took root. During my years as Executive Sous Chef of the AAA Four-Diamond Cascabel in San Antonio and other area kitchens, I became even more deeply focused on locally sourced ingredients. The GO TEXAN program and ever-growing Texas wine industry simply solidified my desire to serve my guests the very best the state has to offer.

I am often asked to be the featured chef at food and wine pairing events at vineyards throughout the Texas Hill Country. You'll find many of the recipes for these dishes in this cookbook, and tips on the wines that go best with them. Because winemakers run out of specific vintages—especially the great ones—I have listed general pairing notes. But know this: The dishes in this cookbook pair ideally with Texas wines. I urge you to seek them out and pour them generously.

Bon appétit and enjoy!

Gracias

I'd like to thank the following individuals for their help in creating this cookbook:

Phil West for his unflinching vision and guidance on the entire project;

Tracy Marlowe and Trish McCabe Rawls for using their "Creative Noggins" on every page;

Jennifer Whitney for her artistic eye with our photographs;

Julia Celeste Rosenfeld for her research and writing talents;

Terry Thompson-Anderson for her kind words and professional support;

and my wife Mariana for being the perfect sous chef in the kitchen and ideal partner in life.

A note from Julia Celeste Rosenfeld

For more than 30 years I've been traveling through Texas and eating great food as a dining writer and avid explorer. So when Ross asked me to work with him on this cookbook, I was prepared to face pages of simple Texas recipes. Pleasantly, I discovered complex layers of flavor created by the French techniques of an experienced chef, and the astute simplicity of a professional who understands how to demystify his skills for the honesty of home cookery. I found an even deeper beauty in Texas wines and a greater appreciation of the state's bountiful farms. I rediscovered Texas in these pages and hope you will too.

COOKING TIPS

1. Be prepared

I'm a strong believer in *mise en place*, a French cooking term we Americans might translate as "everything in place and ready to go." Each recipe in this book is written to help you have the ingredients measured and ready before you begin. I strongly urge you to take this simple preparatory step every time you cook, no matter what you cook. There's nothing worse than getting halfway through preparing a dish only to discover you don't have enough of a key ingredient. Dedicate yourself to *mise en place* and you'll save yourself time and worry.

2. Know your ingredients

Some of the recipes include elements you can make in advance and store for future use, like the Cabernet Grill Cajun Seasoning. We've noted the page number for those ingredient recipes within the larger recipe. You can also order some of these items through our online store at www.CabernetGrill.com.

3. Some shortcuts are fine

We make our own stocks and demi-glace at the Cabernet Grill, and if you're up to the task, I encourage you to take the time and make both at home too. However, one shortcut that is not fine is to buy and use pre-chopped garlic. See my notes about this ingredient on page 137. (Pan Seared Pork Cutlets with Roasted Garlic)

4. You don't need to add flour to cream sauces at home

Because you'll be serving your sauce right away, you don't need to stabilize it with flour. The recipes here achieve the right consistency by naturally reducing the cream to thicken the sauce. In addition, the cream sauces in this cookbook are naturally gluten-free, something you can't rely on restaurants to do.

5. Pay attention to the oils called for in my recipes

Extra virgin olive oil is expensive and a silly waste of money if you're sautéing because heating it diminishes the flavor. It is, however, a wonderful way to add earthy flavor to finished dishes. For a sauté, look for oils with high smoke points, such as safflower or sunflower oil, which also won't infuse the food you're sautéing with its own flavor. Use peanut oil when you fry because it handles prolonged high heat really well. Reserve your good EVOO for dressings, Texas Toast and other full-bodied dishes.

6. We use Texas ingredients as often as possible

If you can't bring them home from your trip to Fredericksburg or find Texas goods in your area, search for similar items in your local grocery stores and gourmet markets. You'll probably find local artisanal goat cheese, for example, in your neck of the woods. You may even find your own local peaches or pecans. But we truly believe that unless you live in Texas and use Texas ingredients, you may be missing out on some flavor nuances with your substitutions.

7. Most ingredients are easy to find

If your local grocer or gourmet store doesn't stock unique items called for in a recipe, just Google it. I find you can order most anything from Amazon.

8. Butter, Bacon and Bourbon: The three Bs of culinary bliss

These three magical ingredients are a staple in every kitchen I direct. Adding them simply makes most everything taste better. Just take a little butter and swirl it into a sauce, or add a touch of butter to raw dough, and you'll infuse terrific richness to a dish. Start a soup with a sauté of bacon, or toss some crisp bits into a stuffing to transform "normal" to a smoke-hinted, crunch-textured, full-bodied dish of wonder. And if adding a touch of bourbon doesn't lift your cooking to new heights, then pour generous shares of it for your guests and no one will care if your dishes weren't perfect.

9. **Adjust the seasonings**

You'll notice that most of my recipes end with the instructions to "adjust the seasoning" with kosher salt and freshly ground black pepper. I have two reasons for preferring this direction over exact measurements. First, everyone has their own preference for how much seasoning a dish should have. Secondly, it's very easy to over-season a dish with salt and pepper if you are just following instructions. Why? Some of the elements may have been smaller than called for in the recipes, or perhaps your reduction went further than expected and the flavors are now deeply concentrated. By adjusting the seasoning a little at a time, you'll learn to season appropriately to make each dish taste right according to the process you used. Remember, you and your guests can always add more seasoning, but you can't take it out. My call for "freshly ground" pepper is important too. Keep a peppermill in your kitchen and on your table and discover the amazing flavor you get from freshly ground pepper. It's an astounding change from pre-ground versions.

A NOTE ABOUT KOSHER SALT

Kosher salt is readily available, and compared to table salt, has a pure taste without any chemical undertones. Another major benefit of kosher over table salt is that you can see and feel it on the food. When I was an apprentice cook at the Weston in Dallas many years ago, we kept a bucket of sugar under the work station where we prepared soufflés, and we would just bend down and grab a handful of sugar to add to the batter. One day, the sugar bucket got switched with a bucket of table salt and every soufflé came back to the kitchen until we realized what was wrong. That's when we switched to kosher salt only so we'd be able to see the difference between the two. I've never gone back to table salt since.

AND ABOUT SEA SALT

Sea salt has made a huge entrance into the cooking world recently, and you can use it instead of kosher salt if you like. It costs a lot more than kosher salt though, so consider using it as a nice finishing touch instead of as a standard ingredient.

When guests arrive, nothing says "welcome" better than a glass of wine and a few nice appetizers. At the Cabernet Grill, we set the tone with Texas wines and simply delicious starters loaded with fresh Texas ingredients.

APPETIZERS

★★★★★

★★★★★

RAMEKINS OF VINE RIPE TOMATOES

with Hill Country Goat Cheese and Texas Toast | Serves 4–6

This dish really shines in the summer when tomatoes and basil are both at their peak.

Ingredients:

2 cups ripe tomatoes, peeled and roughly chopped
¼ cup extra virgin olive oil
1 tablespoon balsamic vinegar
1 tablespoon Worcestershire sauce
2 teaspoons Dijon mustard
1 tablespoon shallots, minced
2 teaspoons garlic, minced
2 tablespoons fresh basil leaves, chiffonade cut
Kosher salt and freshly ground black pepper
4 ounces local goat cheese, crumbled
2 cloves garlic, peeled
3 tablespoons extra virgin olive oil
1 loaf crusty peasant bread, thickly sliced

Preparation:

For the ramekins:

1. Preheat oven broiler.

2. Mix the tomatoes, oil, vinegar, Worcestershire, mustard, shallots, garlic and basil in a large bowl. Taste, and adjust seasoning with salt and pepper.

3. Spoon tomato mixture into small ramekins and top the mixture evenly with goat cheese.

4. Place ramekins under broiler, heating until the cheese starts to bubble and brown lightly.

For the toast:

1. Place the garlic cloves in a small saucer and mash with olive oil.

2. Brush garlic/oil mixture on one side of each slice of bread.

3. Grill or broil bread with oily side to flame until toasted.

DISH ASSEMBLY: *Serve each ramekin on a large plate with a slice or two of toast on the side. Sprinkle the toast with any additional basil you may have for an extra pop of flavor.*

Chiffonade Cut

Create elegant, uniform strips of any leaf using this quick technique. Not only is it fast and uniform, a chiffonade will help retain the natural oils, and flavor, of herbs.

Stack about 10 leaves into a neat, flat pile, all facing the same way.

Roll the stack lengthwise into a tight "cigar" roll with the dark green side out.

Use a very sharp knife to cut the roll from top to bottom, creating thin strips. Use a rocking motion when you cut to avoid bruising the leaves.

Fluff with your fingers. Voila!

CKC FARMS GOAT CHEESE

CKC Farms, in Blanco, Texas, produces one of my favorite artisanal goat cheeses. Aside from great texture and taste, what makes this handmade cheese special is the passion behind it. Chrissy Omo started raising goats and making cheese when she was just 16 years old. Between learning about raising goats and perfecting the craft of cheese-making, Chrissy managed to get a college degree and build a successful business. That's true Hill Country grit! Use artisanal goat cheese from your region in this lusty dish and discover the passion of your local producers.

CKC FARMS
Grade "A" Goat Dairy
BLANCO, TEXAS

GRILLED PEACHES & SHRIMP WITH CREAM
Serves 4

Use slightly firm peaches for this recipe so they hold up to the marinade and heat. If you only have soft, ripe peaches, freeze them for a few minutes after they're marinated before you put them on the grill. If your grill has wide spaces between the grates, you may want to skewer the peach slices and shrimp first, so you don't lose any ingredients to the fire.

Ingredients:

1 pound semi-firm Fredericksburg peaches, peeled, cut into 8 slices
1 tablespoon brown sugar
½ teaspoon Mexican vanilla extract
½ teaspoon pasilla chile powder
1 teaspoon kosher salt
½ teaspoon freshly ground black pepper
½ fresh jalapeño, minced
1 tablespoon fresh cilantro, minced (divided use)
1 tablespoon fresh basil, minced (divided use)
1 pound jumbo Texas wild-caught shrimp, peeled and deveined
1 piece fresh ginger root (2 tablespoons peeled and sliced)
1½ tablespoons freshly-squeezed lemon juice
½ cup heavy cream
Kosher salt and freshly ground black pepper
Safflower oil

Preparation:

For the shrimp and peaches:

1. Preheat charcoal or gas grill to medium heat.

2. Brush the grill surface with safflower oil to reduce sticking.

3. In a small bowl, toss peaches with brown sugar, vanilla, chile powder, salt, pepper, jalapeño and half of the herbs. Allow the peaches to marinate on the counter for at least 15 minutes.

4. Season shrimp with a little salt and pepper.

5. Place shrimp and peaches on preheated grill and cook for about 3 minutes on each side or until shrimp turn pink and start to curl slightly. When cooked, remove to a warm platter.

For the cream:

1. Pour the cream, lemon juice and ginger into a small saucepan set on a medium-high heat. Bring quickly to a full simmer, then remove from heat.

2. Use a slotted spoon to remove and discard the ginger slices from the cream. Taste the cream and season with a little salt and pepper.

DISH ASSEMBLY: *Distribute shrimp and peaches evenly among 4 bowls, then pour hot cream over the fruit/shrimp mixture. Sprinkle with remaining cilantro and basil. Serve warm.*

FREDERICKSBURG PEACHES

German settlers who came to this part of Texas around 1864 discovered that the climate and soil of their new home was ideal for peaches. Now 40% of Texas' peaches are grown here in the Hill Country — specifically in Gillespie County where Fredericksburg is located.

Hill Country peaches have such a following that fans drive for hours to get them here. If you visit us between May and August, stop at a roadside stand and wrestle a few from the locals. Texas may not be America's top peach producer, but the state still grows enough top-notch fruit to do itself proud. And once you taste the sweetness, you'll understand why Fredericksburg peaches have such a good reputation.

If you're lucky enough to book a room here at the Cotton Gin Village on the third weekend in June, you won't want to miss the Peach JAMboree and Rodeo in neighboring Stonewall, where you'll get a memorable taste of peaches and Texas hospitality.

Texas
Hill Country
Peaches

Buying fresh peaches from an orchard stand is the easy way out, but not nearly as much fun as picking your own. Several of the 20 grower/members in the Hill Country Fruit Council open their orchards each season so you can pick your own fine fruit from their trees.

The early varieties that ripen from about May 10 into early June are "cling" peaches, with flesh that clings to the craggy pit. The next crop to ripen in June are "semi-freestone" peaches, and finally, the popular "freestone" varieties are ready from mid-June through late July and often well into August.

Keep fresh peaches at room temperature until they're soft and ready to eat. Once they're soft, store them in the refrigerator for up to two weeks (if they last that long!). To freeze them for later: Peel and slice them; lay the slices on a baking sheet; place the baking sheet in the freezer for at least 4 hours; then transfer the frozen slices to an airtight plastic bag. They'll keep in the freezer for up to 6 months.

POBLANO RAJAS CON CREMA
Serves 6

This is one of my all-time favorite recipes, and it's not one for the timid palate. It is an excessively rich and wonderful appetizer, and it can also be used as a sauce for foods that are a bit dry, like grilled chicken breast or pork chops. However, my favorite way to serve (and eat) it is to simply spoon the mixture into a hot, fresh flour tortilla, top it with a little minced cilantro and fresh serrano chile, and roll it up. Your taste buds will "sting" with delight!

Ingredients:

Cooking oil spray
4 fresh poblano chiles
½ tablespoon safflower oil
1 clove garlic, minced
½ cup chicken stock
½ cup heavy cream
6 ounces cream cheese, softened
3 ounces Oaxaca or Monterrey Jack cheese, grated
2 tablespoons fresh cilantro leaves, washed
  and chopped
2 fresh serrano chiles, minced
6 flour tortillas

Roasting Chiles

The word "rajas" loosely translates to "slits," but as a culinary term, it is the by-product of roasting fresh chiles over fire until their skin blisters, then removing the skin and seeds, and cutting the chile into long strips. These versatile strips, or "rajas," are a staple in many Mexican dishes and you'll see I use them in other recipes in this book.

Fire-roasting imparts a smoky essence to chiles and is an important element in the deep flavors of Mexico. When you peel off the skin of the chiles, you reduce possible bitterness. The heat resides in the seeds and membrane of most chiles (not poblano or bell peppers, which are mild), so if you are working with hotter chiles like jalapeños or serranos, keep that in mind and adjust accordingly.

Preparation:

1. Preheat grill or broiler to high.

2. Spray all sides of the poblanos with cooking oil, and place on grill or under broiler.

3. Turn the chiles to allow the skin to blister and blacken on all sides, being careful to avoid charring the tender flesh.

4. When the skin is blistered, place the hot chiles in small bowl and cover with a damp towel for 2–5 minutes. This will help you easily remove the skins.

5. When cooled slightly, remove the blistered skin, seeds and stems. You may want to wear thin rubber gloves and use a damp pastry brush to help with the job. Avoid running the chiles under water.

6. Cut the cleaned chile flesh into long ¼-inch-wide strips and set aside.

7. In a small saucepan, heat the safflower oil to medium. Add the garlic and sauté briefly.

8. Add the chicken stock and cream, bring to a boil, then reduce heat to low.

9. Lightly whisk in cream cheese and Oaxaca cheese to a smooth, warm consistency.

CHEF'S NOTE: *The silkiness of this dish can be lost if you heat the mixture to too high of a temperature, causing the oils in both the cream and cheeses to separate. Heat it gently enough to melt all the cheese, but not quickly or at such a high temperature that it simmers or boils.*

10. Mix in chile strips and pour into a small serving bowl, keeping it warm until ready to serve.

DISH ASSEMBLY: *Individually heat flour tortillas in a dry skillet, keeping the warmed stack wrapped in a damp towel or tortilla holder until ready to serve. Spoon Poblano Rajas con Crema into hot tortillas, top with cilantro and minced serrano, roll up, and serve.*

CRISPY ASIAGO CRUSTED EGGPLANT

Serves 4

I don't like to waste anything. So when we found ourselves with lots of eggplant trimmings from our Cajun Eggplant Pirogue entrée (page 112), I thought we should do something with them. Now this appetizer is so popular we use whole eggplants, not just the trimmings.

Ingredients:

Peanut oil for frying
¼ cup all-purpose flour
½ teaspoon Cabernet Grill Cajun Seasoning
1 egg, lightly beaten
¼ cup milk
¾ cup Panko breadcrumbs
¼ cup + 2 tablespoons Asiago cheese, freshly grated
1 tablespoon fresh parsley, minced
1 medium size eggplant
2 tablespoons Mango Chutney Mayo (see recipe)

Mango Chutney Mayo

Yield: 1 cup

Ingredients:

¾ cup mayonnaise
3 tablespoons Major Grey's Mango Chutney
   (any brand)
2 teaspoons Sriracha Sauce

Preparation:

1. Place all ingredients in a small food processor and purée.

2. Refrigerate until ready to use.

Preparation:

1. If you don't have a deep fryer, use a heavy-bottomed pot. Pour in enough oil to come at least 2 inches up the side of the pot. Preheat oil to 350°.

2. Set up a breading station with 3 bowls: Mix together flour and seasoning in the first bowl; Mix together the egg and the milk in the second; Mix together the Panko breadcrumbs, cheese and parsley in the third.

3. Trim off the ends of the eggplant and slice the rest into ½-inch thick medallions. If you prefer your eggplant peeled, go right ahead.

4. Bread each eggplant medallion—first in the flour mixture, shaking off excess flour; then coating the medallion in the egg wash, draining off excess liquid; and finally coating it in the Panko mix, covering each slice completely and evenly.

5. Test the fryer oil by dropping a pinch of breadcrumbs into the oil. It's at the right temperature if the oil bubbles rapidly around the edges of the breadcrumbs and they turn a golden color.

6. Working in batches, drop the breaded eggplant medallions into the fryer, cooking about 1–2 minutes on each side, or until golden brown and crispy.

7. Remove the crispy medallions from the fryer to a warm platter lined with paper towels to absorb excess oil. Season immediately with a sprinkle of Cabernet Grill Cajun Seasoning.

DISH ASSEMBLY: *Place finished eggplant on a large serving platter, drizzle with Mango Mayo and sprinkle with 2 tablespoons of grated Asiago cheese.*

It's worth seeking out the excellent goat cheeses from both Pure Luck Farm & Dairy and CKC Farms when you visit the Texas Hill Country. Because of the volume of cheese we use at the Cabernet Grill Texas Wine Country Restaurant, we serve a commercially-produced goat cheese from Cleveland, Texas, but I use both Pure Luck and CKC cheeses at home. You can make this recipe in small ovenproof ramekins for individual servings, or bake it in a large soufflé dish and set it in the middle of the dining table or on a buffet.

Ingredients:

⅛ cup sundried tomatoes, chopped
2 teaspoons fresh rosemary, minced
1 teaspoon fresh oregano, minced
¼ cup extra virgin olive oil
½ cup kalamata olives, pitted and chopped
20 or more cloves roasted garlic
8 ounces Texas goat cheese
1 long baguette, sliced and toasted

Preparation:

1. Mix together sundried tomatoes, herbs, olive oil and olives in a small bowl. Set aside and allow to marinate for at least 15 minutes.

2. Crumble goat cheese into ramekins or soufflé dish. Top cheese with roasted garlic cloves, then the marinated olive mixture.

3. Move ramekins to a baking tray and place in a 350° oven for 10–15 minutes, or until goat cheese is warm all the way through. If you are using a single large soufflé dish, increase the cooking time and watch as it bakes to avoid burning.

4. Serve warm with slices of toasted baguette.

Wine Accompaniments

I like to serve glasses of chilled McPherson Cellars Viognier or a Sandstone Cellars red (especially Sandstone Cellars V, if it's available) with this dish. The dry taste and sweet aroma of white Viognier complement the herbal saltiness of this dish, while the long finish of Sandstone's reds, particularly V, harmonizes with the rustic, creamy cheese.

JUMBO LUMP CRAB GRATIN
Serves 4

If you have escargot dishes in your cabinet, you either use them all the time or never. There's no in-between. If you're in the "never" camp, this dish may switch you over to the "all the time" side. Your guests will love this appetizer, and you will love how simple it is to make. Don't have escargot dishes? Use the smallest ramekins you have.

Ingredients:

1 stick unsalted butter, at room temperature
2 teaspoons Sambal Oelek (also called
  Sambal Ulek)
½ teaspoon freshly-squeezed lemon juice
Pinch kosher salt
Pinch freshly ground black pepper
½ pound jumbo lump blue crab meat
½ cup Asiago cheese, freshly grated, divided into
  4 portions
2 teaspoons dry breadcrumbs, divided into
  4 portions
2 lemons, cut into 8 wedges

Preparation:

1. Preheat oven to 375°.

2. Mix soft butter, Sambal, lemon juice, salt and pepper in a small bowl.

3. Using 4 6-hole escargot dishes, fill each hole with one lump of crab meat and top with about a ½ teaspoon or so of the butter mixture. If you have any crab or butter left over, continue to divide it evenly among the dishes.

4. Sprinkle cheese equally on top of each escargot pocket. Follow with equal sprinkles of breadcrumbs.

5. Bake for about 18 minutes or until the tops of the dish are golden brown and bubbly.

6. Serve hot with lemon wedges.

Sambal Oelek

"Sambal" is a catch-all phrase for more than 300 varieties of chile-based sauces found in Indonesia and throughout Asia. They're always hot and pack a punch. What I like about Sambal Oelek is that it doesn't contain any extra garlic, spices or fish sauce that might overpower other flavors in a dish. It's heavenly heat in its purest form. You'll find it in many large grocery stores, Asian specialty food stores, and, of course, online.

TITO'S TIPSY TEXAS SHRIMP COCKTAIL
Serves 4

Please don't overcook shrimp. I say this as an advocate for Texas wild-caught shrimp and a lover of fine food. I cringe when I read recipes that call for boiling shrimp for 10 minutes when all you need is 2 minutes per pound of shelled shrimp (3-4 minutes/pound for shell-on). More than that and your shrimp will be rubbery.

Ingredients:
1 pound large Texas wild-caught shrimp, peeled and deveined
3 cups water
1 tablespoon Cabernet Grill Cajun Seasoning
1 red bell pepper, thinly sliced
½ cup red onions, very thinly sliced
1 shallot, peeled and minced
1 clove garlic, minced
½ jalapeño, seeded and minced
2 tablespoons freshly-squeezed lime juice
1 cup Bloody Bull Mix (see recipe)
1 shot Tito's Handmade Vodka
2 small avocados
Kosher salt and freshly ground black pepper
8 jumbo jalapeño-stuffed olives
4 chilled martini glasses
4 lemon wedges

Preparation:
1. Place water in a medium saucepot over high heat. Add Cabernet Grill Cajun Seasoning and bring to a boil.

2. Add shrimp and cook for about 1–2 minutes (no longer) until they turn pink, start to curl a little, and the center is no longer translucent.

3. Drain the shrimp, move to a cool platter and place in the refrigerator to chill.

4. When ready to serve, mix the red bell pepper, red onions, shallot, garlic, jalapeño, lime, Bloody Bull Mix and vodka in a small bowl. Add cooled shrimp and season with salt and pepper.

Bloody Bull Mix
You can keep this mixture refrigerated for up to 5 days. It adds spice to this shrimp cocktail and is ideal as a Bloody Mary mix.

Ingredients:
2½ cups tomato juice
2½ cups beef consommé
2 tablespoons Worcestershire sauce
1 tablespoon prepared horseradish
2 teaspoons Tabasco Sauce
¼ cup freshly-squeezed lime juice
1½ teaspoons Cabernet Grill Cajun Seasoning

Preparation:
1. Mix all ingredients and refrigerate until chilled.

DISH ASSEMBLY: *Divide shrimp mixture evenly between 4 large margarita or martini glasses. Peel and cut the avocado into quarters, season slices with a little salt and pepper, and place a slice on top of each martini glass. Top the shrimp with 2 olives and a wedge of lemon.*

TEXAS BLUE CRAB SALSA

with Tostadas (AKA Pico de Crab) | Serves 4–6

Serve this dish instead of plain chips and salsa when you want to make an impression, and there will be no doubt you know how to cook first-class finger food with Texas panache. Texas blue crabs provide some of the most succulent crab meat available. You can normally purchase pre-cooked meat in 1-pound containers, and in various grades based on the part of the crab the meat is pulled from, and how many shell fragments remain after processing. The grading also determines the price, with jumbo lump meat at the top of desirability and price scale— because it is the best by far. Decide what grade to use based on your budget.

Ingredients:

1 cup jumbo lump Texas blue crab meat
3 ripe tomatoes, peeled and cut into a medium dice
3 green onions, minced
¼ cup celery, minced
4 serrano chiles, minced
¼ cup fresh cilantro, minced
1 tablespoon freshly-squeezed lime juice
Kosher salt and freshly ground black pepper
1 bowl warm corn tortilla chips

Preparation:

1. Pick through crab meat carefully to remove all shell fragments, while trying to keep the meat in large lumps.

2. Place all ingredients (except for chips) in a small bowl and mix together.

3. Adjust seasoning with salt and pepper, cover and refrigerate until chilled and ready to serve.

4. Serve with tortilla chips warm from the oven.

CHEF'S NOTE: *Fresh crab has a short shelf life, so serve this the same day you make it.*

CHARBROILED LOCKHART QUAIL
with Malted Jalapeño Waffles and Cayenne Honey Glaze | Serves 4

This is an appetizer version of Hill Country chicken and waffles, where everyone gets their own small bird. I served this dish as part of a vintner dinner at Grape Creek Vineyards pairing it with Cabernet Blanc, a quintessential Texas semi-sweet Rosé. The hints of berries and honeysuckle in that wine may move you away from White Zinfandel forever.

Ingredients:

4 semi-boneless quails
4 slices applewood smoked bacon
Kosher salt and freshly ground black pepper
½ cup local honey
¼ teaspoon cayenne pepper
1 cup Carbon's Golden Malted Pancake &
    Waffle Flour
1 egg
2 tablespoons unsalted butter, melted
5 ounces water
2 tablespoons sliced candied jalapeños,
    roughly chopped
3 tablespoons unsalted butter, room temperature

Preparation:

1. Preheat both a waffle maker and a charcoal or gas grill.

For the quail:

1. Wrap each quail with a strip of bacon and secure with a toothpick.

2. Season quail with salt and pepper, place on preheated grill and cook for about 6 minutes per side, until the quail is fully cooked. When done, the juices should run clear, and the meat should no longer be pink when pierced with a small knife.

3. Remove the quail to a warm platter, remove the toothpicks and keep warm until ready to serve.

For the glaze:

1. Place honey and cayenne pepper in a small bowl and whisk together until well combined.

For the waffles:

1. In a medium bowl, mix together the flour, egg, melted butter and water until almost smooth. Add the candied jalapeños and stir.

2. Pour half the mixture into a well-greased Belgian waffle iron and cook until golden brown and crisp. Repeat to make a second waffle.

3. Liberally spread waffles with butter, then cut waffles into quarters.

DISH ASSEMBLY: *Place 2 waffle quarters on each plate and top with the cooked quail. Drizzle both the quail and the waffles with Cayenne Honey Glaze. Serve immediately.*

CHEF'S NOTE: *When I find something that works, I stick with it for years. That's the case with Carbon's waffle flour. It consistently delivers flavorful, crisp waffles from a foolproof recipe. It used to only be available for professional kitchens in hotels and country clubs, but I've seen it on consumer shelves recently at a variety of markets. And, of course, online.*

SPICY SPINACH AND TEXAS WILD-CAUGHT SHRIMP BEIGNETS

with Basil Remoulade | Serves 8–12

New Orleans meets the Texas Hill Country in this memorable appetizer.

Ingredients:

2 packed cups fresh spinach leaves, stems removed
1 tablespoon olive oil
1 pound Texas wild-caught shrimp, peeled, deveined, roughly chopped
¼ cup green onions, minced
1½ cups all-purpose flour
1 teaspoon baking powder
¾ cup milk
2 teaspoons freshly-squeezed lemon juice
1 fresh jalapeño, minced
1 whole egg, slightly beaten
2 egg whites
Peanut or safflower oil for frying
Cabernet Grill Cajun Seasoning
Basil Remoulade (see recipe)

Preparation:

1. If you don't have a deep fryer, use a heavy-bottomed pot. Pour in enough peanut or safflower oil to come at least 2 inches up the side of the pot. Preheat oil to 375°.

2. Heat the olive oil in a small skillet over medium heat. Add the spinach and sauté until wilted. Remove from the heat and allow spinach to cool in the pan.

3. Move cooled spinach to a dish towel and wring out as much liquid as possible. Chop the spinach roughly.

4. In a large bowl, place spinach, shrimp, green onions, flour, baking powder, milk, lemon juice, jalapeño and slightly beaten egg. Mix all ingredients with a spoon until a batter forms. Do not over-mix.

5. Place the egg whites in a clean bowl and whip until they form soft peaks. Fold the egg white mixture into the batter.

6. Use a small dough scoop or tablespoon to drop scoops of the batter into the hot oil. Fry about 4 minutes, turning occasionally until the beignets are golden brown and floating.

7. Drain on paper towels and season with a bit of Cabernet Grill Cajun Seasoning while still warm.

Basil Remoulade

Makes 1½ cups

Ingredients:

1 packed cup fresh basil leaves, stems removed
1 packed cup spinach leaves, stems removed
2 tablespoons olive oil
1 cup mayonnaise
1 teaspoon Tabasco Sauce
2 teaspoons Creole or Dijon mustard
1 teaspoon fresh garlic, minced
1 pinch freshly ground black pepper

Preparation:

1. Heat the olive oil in a small skillet over medium heat. Add the basil and spinach; sauté until wilted. Remove from the heat and allow to cool in the pan.

2. Place the wilted greens in a dish towel and wring out as much liquid as possible.

3. Place the spinach, basil and remaining ingredients in a small food processor and puree until the sauce is green and smooth.

4. Refrigerate in a serving bowl until beignets are ready.

DISH ASSEMBLY: *Place drained beignets on a platter and season with a few more sprinkles of Cabernet Grill Cajun Seasoning if desired. Place the bowl of Basil Remoulade beside the platter as a dipping sauce.*

TASSO RABBIT CAKES
with Rio Red Grapefruit Beurre Blanc, Scallion Coulis and Radish Slaw
Serves 6

52

People are funny about eating rabbit. Actually, they're funny about eating a lot of things. But rabbit has long been part of the American diet, and it was once as common to see rabbit on a family dining table as it was to see chicken. It's got a delicious, mild flavor and very little fat, so it's both satisfying and healthy. Bottom line: Avoid any controversy at your table and only tell your guests they ate rabbit after you clear the plates.

Tasso Rabbit Cakes
Yield: 12 cakes

Ingredients:
2 cups Cajun Braised Rabbit, shredded (see recipe)
2 egg yolks
½ cup Tasso ham, ⅛-inch dice
2 green onions, minced
1 tablespoon celery, minced
1½ tablespoon Zatarain's Creole mustard
½ cup mayonnaise
1 teaspoon Tabasco Sauce
Cabernet Grill Cajun Seasoning
½ cup all-purpose flour
1 whole egg, lightly beaten
¾ cup milk
1 cup Panko breadcrumbs
3 tablespoons safflower oil

Preparation:
1. Place the braised rabbit, egg yolks, Tasso ham, green onions, celery, mustard, mayo and Tabasco in a medium size bowl. Mix until well incorporated.

2. Taste the mixture to see if it needs seasoning, though the Tasso ham and braising liquid reduction from the rabbit should provide enough flavor. If it needs a bit more, add additional Cabernet Grill Cajun Seasoning.

3. Roll the mixture into 12 equal portions, each about the size of a golf ball. Flatten each ball a bit between the palms of your hands until they are each about ¾-inch thick and about 2½ inches in diameter.

4. Set up a breading station with 3 bowls: Mix together flour and one teaspoon of Cabernet Grill seasoning in the first bowl; Mix together the egg and the milk in the second; Place the breadcrumbs in the third. Bread each rabbit cake—first in the flour mixture, shaking off excess flour; then in a coating of egg wash, draining off excess liquid; and finally coating it in an even covering of Panko. Place each breaded cake on a plate until all are prepared for the next step.

5. Heat a large skillet over medium heat and add the safflower oil. Place the cakes in the pan in a single layer (you may need to cook in batches), and sauté for about 4 minutes on each side or until golden brown and hot all the way through. Drain on paper towels before plating.

DISH ASSEMBLY: *Set 2 cakes on each plate and spoon a bit of the Grapefruit Beurre Blanc sauce around each set of cakes. Top the cakes with a spoonful of the Radish Slaw, then drizzle the Scallion Coulis around the plate.*

Cajun Braised Rabbit
Yield: About 2 cups of pulled meat

Ingredients:
2½–3 pounds whole rabbit (often in freezer
    section of grocery meat departments)
1 tablespoon Cabernet Grill Cajun Seasoning
2 tablespoons safflower oil
½ cup yellow onions, roughly chopped
½ cup carrot, roughly chopped
¼ cup celery, roughly chopped
4 cloves garlic, smashed
1 bay leaf
½ teaspoon fresh thyme
1 fresh jalapeño, sliced
⅓ cup Herbsaint Liqueur or other anise liqueur
½ cup fresh tomato, chopped
3 cups chicken stock or water

Preparation:
1. Preheat oven to 350°.

2. Cut the rabbit into 4 pieces, pat dry and season both sides with
Cajun seasoning.

3. Heat a large heavy-bottomed pot or Dutch oven over medium-high heat.
Add the safflower oil, then add the rabbit pieces, browning the meat
very well on one side before turning and browning the other side.

4. Remove the rabbit to a plate and set aside. Add the onions, carrot and
celery to the pot, browning the vegetables a bit on each side.

5. Remove the pot from the heat and place the rabbit back in the pot. Add
the remaining ingredients and cover tightly with a lid or heavy duty foil.
Place the pot in the preheated oven to braise for 1¼ hours or until the
rabbit meat is tender and falling off the bone when tested.

6. Allow the rabbit to cool in the braising liquid. Once cool, remove the
rabbit to a bowl and pull the meat from the bones, discarding any
cartilage or gristle.

7. Strain the braising liquid and pour it into a saucepan set over medium-
high heat. Allow the liquid to reduce until there is only about ½ cup or
less remaining. Pour the reduction over the pulled rabbit meat.

8. Refrigerate until ready to use.

Rio Red Grapefruit Beurre Blanc
Yield: 1 cup

This versatile sauce is also delicious with grilled shrimp or broiled grouper. Use a stainless steel saucepan when preparing this recipe, otherwise the sauce can turn an unappetizing color when whisked.

Ingredients:
2 shallots, minced
1 tablespoon Safflower oil
2 cups freshly-squeezed Texas ruby red grapefruit juice
1 teaspoon fresh grapefruit zest
1½ sticks cold unsalted butter, cut into cubes
Kosher salt and freshly ground black pepper

Preparation:
1. Add the safflower oil to a small stainless steel saucepan set on medium
heat. Sweat the shallots very slowly until soft and translucent, being sure
they don't brown.

2. Add the grapefruit juice to the pan and turn the heat to high, bringing
the juice to a boil. Lower the heat to medium-high and allow the juice to
reduce by about 80% so that it starts to thicken like a glaze.

3. Remove the pan from the heat and begin to whisk in the butter, a few
cubes at a time, to form a creamy sauce. If the butter is not melting, put
the saucepan back on the heat just briefly to warm the sauce back up.

   CHEF'S NOTE: *If you get the sauce too hot, the butter will "break" and you
   will have an oily mess on your hands. At that point, you'll need to start over.*

4. Once all the butter is incorporated into the reduction, strain the sauce
through a fine sieve and discard the shallots.

5. Adjust the seasoning with salt and pepper. Serve immediately.

Scallion Coulis

Yield: About ½ cup

Ingredients:

6 green onions, top green part only
1 small handful fresh baby spinach
⅓ cup chicken stock, warm
Kosher salt and freshly ground black pepper

What is a Coulis?

These fruit or vegetable purees are either sweet or savory and add a pop of color and flavor as a garnish. It's pronounced "cool-ee" with the emphasis on the last syllable.

Preparation:

1. Bring about 3 inches of water to a boil in a medium size sauce pan.

2. Prepare an ice bath by filling a large bowl with ice cubes and cold water.

3. Drop the green onions and spinach into the boiling water and allow them to steep for about 30 seconds or until bright green.

4. Immediately drain the onions and spinach from the boiling water and plunge them into the ice bath for a few seconds to stop the cooking. Remove the vegetables to a colander and allow to drain.

5. Once drained, place the vegetables in the bowl of a food processor and add the chicken stock. Process until fully pureed.

6. Adjust seasoning with salt and pepper.

Radish Slaw

Yield: About ¾ cup

This slaw wilts quickly, so make it just prior to serving. It's a potent salad, so use it lightly as a garnish.

Ingredients:

1½ cups French breakfast radish or other long radish variety, trimmed
2 teaspoons champagne vinegar
2 tablespoons sugar
2 teaspoons fresh chives, minced
1 pinch grated lemon zest
Kosher salt and freshly ground black pepper

Preparation:

1. Using a mandolin slicer with the julienne blade set for very fine cut; julienne the radish and place in a small bowl.

2. Mix together the remaining ingredients and season with salt and pepper.

Texas Ruby Red Grapefruit

I'm a true believer in the glory of Texas Rio Star and Ruby-Sweet Grapefruit—so sweet and juicy that I can no longer eat any other variety. Even when I visit my parents in Florida, I just say "no thanks" to their local pink. What makes Texas rubies so wonderful is that they're tree-ripened, hand-picked and the prettiest color red you'll ever see. Growers in the Rio Grande Valley have been perfecting the crop since the 1920s. In 1993, the Texas red grapefruit was designated the official state fruit of Texas.

Every season calls for soup, whether it's to warm up from a chill or cool down from the heat. Crowd-pleasing and easy to serve, these soups pour a touch of originality into every bowl turning "soup" into "super."

SOUPS

★ ★ ★ ★ ★

★ ★ ★ ★ ★

HILL COUNTRY BUTTERMILK PEACH SOUP
Serves 4–6 as an appetizer

I've often wondered why most Texans don't order cold soups. I've put this refreshing soup on the menu a number of times and it just doesn't sell well. But if I send out free samples, everyone tells me it should be on the menu every day! Fredericksburg peaches are at their peak when Texas temperatures start rising—so this is a great dish for beating the heat.

Ingredients:

1½ cups buttermilk
¾ cup heavy cream
1 teaspoon fresh orange zest
1 ounce freshly-squeezed lime juice
6 medium Fredericksburg peaches, peeled, pitted and pureed
¼ cup granulated sugar
1 cup apple juice
⅛ cup dry Sherry
2 teaspoons candied jalapeños, minced (optional)
2 tablespoons toasted pecans, chopped

Preparation:

1. Mix all ingredients, except jalapeños and pecans, and chill in refrigerator for a few hours.

2. Place soup cups and spoons in refrigerator to chill.

3. Serve soup in chilled cups and garnish with candied jalapeño and pecans.

SWEET AND SPICY

I've talked to a lot of chefs who share my views on candied jalapeños: they're pretty addictive. These sugar-brined slices of fresh jalapeños and garlic chunks pump up dips, burgers, soups, baked goods — you name it. I just like them straight from the jar. It's candy for chile heads like me.

PASILLA CHILE & GRILLED QUAIL TORTILLA SOUP
Serves 6–8

Quail is a staple on many Texas tables, especially here in the Hill Country where people often hunt for their own. Farm-raised quail is plentiful around here too, offering chefs and home cooks a locally sourced, low-fat, great-tasting bird without the gaminess of duck or dove. If you can't find quail in your area, a Cornish hen makes a good substitute.

Ingredients:

2 tablespoons safflower oil
1 cup yellow onions, medium dice
2 tablespoons garlic, minced
3 white corn tortillas, medium dice
2 tablespoons ground pasilla chile powder
¼ teaspoon cayenne pepper
1 tablespoon ground cumin
½ tablespoon ground coriander seed
½ teaspoon freshly ground black pepper
3 cups chicken stock
2 cups brown veal stock
1 cup tomatoes, peeled and chopped
½ cup poblano rajas
2 cups grilled boneless quail breast meat, diced
Kosher salt
6 white corn tortillas, cut in ¼-inch wide strips
Peanut oil
1 cup queso añejo, crumbled
1 avocado, medium dice

Preparation:

1. Over medium heat in a heavy pot, sauté onions in oil until nearly translucent.

2. Add garlic and diced corn tortillas and continue to sauté for about 1 minute.

3. Add chile powder, cayenne pepper, cumin, coriander and pepper, as you sauté for another minute or until fragrant.

4. Add tomatoes and both stocks, increase heat to high, and bring the mixture to a boil.

5. Once boiling, reduce heat immediately and simmer for 20 minutes.

6. Add poblano strips and diced quail. Simmer another 10 minutes.

7. Check seasoning and add salt accordingly.

8. Heat a small sauté or frying pan with at least 1 inch of peanut oil to 350°, add tortilla strips and fry until crisp. Drain tortilla strips on paper towels and season with salt and pepper.

9. Ladle soup into warmed bowls and top with tortilla strips, cheese and avocado.

CHEF'S NOTE: *If you don't have both chicken and veal stock available, use one or the other for a total of 5 cups.*

JUMBO LUMP CRAB WITH AVOCADO AND COCONUT CURRY LIME BROTH

Serves 4

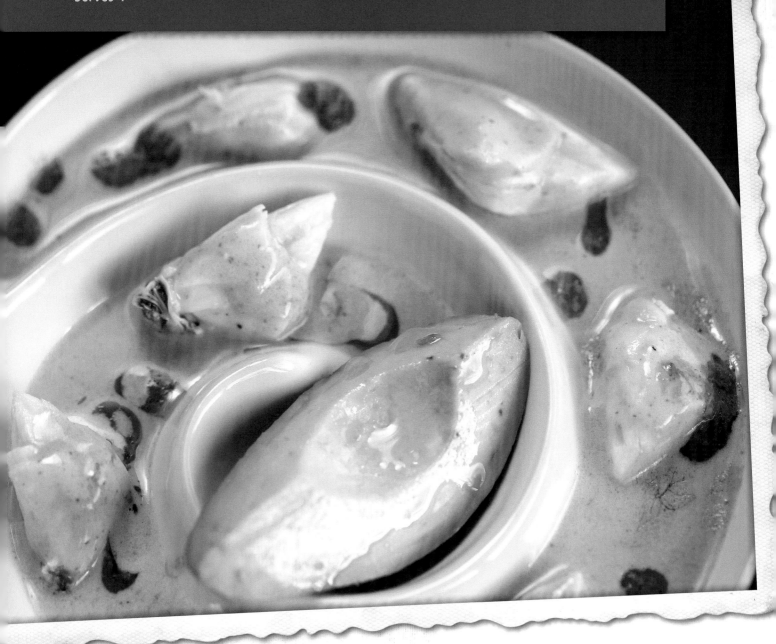

This dish was created for a Cuvee Blanc pairing during a vintner dinner with Grape Creek Vineyards. I like the Asian flavors this soup evokes, making it an unusual twist on Hill Country dining. The crispness of the Cuvee Blanc, a blend of mostly Pinot Grigio and Viognier, acts as a nice counterpoint to the creaminess of the dish and sets off the flavor of the crab and avocado.

Ingredients:
½ cup yellow onions, diced
2 cloves garlic, minced
2 shallots, minced
3 tablespoons fresh ginger, minced
2 tablespoons safflower oil
1½ tablespoons madras curry powder
2 (13.5 oz.) cans coconut milk, unsweetened
1½ tablespoons freshly-squeezed lime juice
Kosher salt and white pepper
1 cup jumbo lump blue crab meat
1 small avocado, peeled and cut in quarters
½ cup Scallion Coulis (see recipe)

Preparation:
1. In a medium pot over medium-low heat, sweat onions, garlic, shallots and ginger in oil for about 8 minutes until translucent, being careful to not brown the vegetables. Add curry powder and sauté briefly until aromatic.

2. Add coconut milk and bring to a boil, then immediately reduce to simmer and cook for about 10 minutes.

3. Add lime juice, then adjust seasoning with salt and white pepper.

4. Strain the onions, garlic and ginger from the soup and discard. Keep soup hot as you prepare the completed dish.

DISH ASSEMBLY: *Divide lump crab and avocado equally in the bottom of each soup bowl. Place bowls in a 350° oven for 3 minutes to heat the bowls, crab and avocado. Pour very hot soup over crab and avocado and serve immediately.*

Scallion Coulis
Yield: About ½ cup

Ingredients:
6 green onions, top green part only
1 small handful fresh baby spinach
⅓ cup chicken stock, warm
Kosher salt and freshly ground black pepper

Preparation:
1. Bring about 3 inches of water to a boil in a medium size sauce pan.

2. Prepare an ice bath in a large bowl by filling it with ice cubes and cold water.

3. Drop the green onions and spinach into the boiling water and allow them to steep for about 30 seconds or until bright green.

4. Immediately drain the onions and spinach from the boiling water and plunge them into the ice bath for a few seconds to stop the cooking. Remove the vegetables to a colander and allow to drain.

5. Once drained, place the vegetables in the bowl of a food processor and add the chicken stock. Process until fully pureed.

6. Adjust seasoning with salt and pepper.

TOMATO BASIL SOUP
Serves 4–6

I love tomato soup for the same reason so many others do. It was a childhood favorite that still puts a smile on my face today. I grew up in Michigan and frequently slogged to and from school in the snow. But the 1-mile walk grew shorter when I knew there would be tomato soup on the kitchen table when I got home for lunch. I think this is an even better version of that comforting food as it incorporates one of the Cabernet Grill's three Bs of ultimate culinary enhancement: Butter, Bourbon, and in this case, Bacon!

Ingredients:
1 tablespoon safflower oil
4 strips bacon, ¼-inch dice
½ cup celery, ¼-inch dice
1 cup onions, ¼-inch dice
2 cloves garlic, minced
2 bay leaves
¼ cup all-purpose flour
4 cups chicken stock
1½ cups heavy cream
2 cups tomato puree
2 tablespoons granulated sugar
¼ cup fresh basil leaves, chiffonade
Kosher salt and freshly ground black pepper

Preparation:
1. Heat a heavy-bottomed saucepot over medium heat and add the oil and bacon.

2. Stir frequently until the bacon begins to brown a bit on its edges and most of the fat has been rendered.

3. Add the celery, onions, garlic and bay leaves and reduce the heat to medium-low. Stir frequently, cooking the vegetables slowly until they soften and the onions become translucent.

4. Add the flour and stir to coat the vegetables evenly.

5. Pour in chicken stock a cup at a time, stirring well after each addition so that no lumps of flour form. Add the cream and tomato puree, stirring well to incorporate.

6. Bring the soup to a boil over high heat for about 2 minutes, then reduce the heat to a simmer for about 20 minutes.

7. Strain the vegetables and bacon from the liquid, or leave them in for a heartier version.

8. Stir in sugar and basil, and adjust seasoning accordingly with salt and pepper.

CHEF'S NOTE: *See page 29 for instructions on how to chiffonade basil.*

CRISPY FRIED TEXAS OYSTER CHOWDER
with Roasted Hatch Chiles | Serves 6

Ingredients:

2 tablespoons safflower oil
4 strips bacon, diced
½ cup yellow onions, ¼-inch dice
½ cup carrots, ¼-inch dice
½ cup celery, ¼-inch dice
1 tablespoon garlic, minced
2 bay leaves
½ teaspoon fresh thyme
1 teaspoon freshly ground black pepper
⅓ cup all-purpose flour
3 cups clam juice, oyster liquor or chicken stock
1 cup heavy cream
1 cup russet potatoes, boiled, peeled and cut in
    ½-inch dice
½ cup roasted and peeled Hatch green chiles,
    deseeded and diced
Kosher salt
1 cup buttermilk
¾ cup cracker meal
⅓ cup dry masa harina
1 tablespoon Cabernet Grill Cajun Seasoning
Peanut oil
18 Texas Gulf oysters, shelled

Texas Gulf Coast Oyster Appellations

The Texas Gulf Coast oystermen are rightfully proud of their mollusks. And, like the subtleties of wines, oyster flavors are developed by the salinity of the waters where they grow. In the wine industry, "appellation" refers to the geographic area where the grapes were grown. If the oyster industry continues on its present course, you should soon be able to select oysters according to their appellation too, defined by the specific Galveston Bay reef where they were harvested. This labeling is designed to assure you of the flavor, size and quality of the oysters you're getting.

Preparation:

1. Heat a heavy-bottomed saucepan over medium heat. Add safflower oil and bacon, cooking until the bacon is browned on the edges and just starting to crisp.

2. Add onions, carrots, celery and garlic, and sauté with the bacon until the vegetables get semi-soft and translucent.

3. Add bay leaves, thyme, pepper and flour, stirring constantly for about 1 minute or until fragrant.

4. Pour in clam juice or stock, 1 cup at a time, stirring with a wire whisk until fully incorporated each time, being sure to whisk away any lumps of flour.

5. Turn the heat to high and bring mixture to a boil. As soon as it boils, reduce the heat back down to a simmer. Allow the chowder to simmer for about 20 minutes on low heat.

6. Add the cream, potatoes and chiles to the chowder, and simmer for another 5–10 minutes, allowing all the flavors to blend.

7. Adjust seasoning with salt. Keep warm until ready to serve.

8. Meanwhile, place the buttermilk and oysters in a small bowl.

9. In another small bowl, mix cracker meal, masa and Cabernet Grill Cajun Seasoning.

10. Add enough peanut oil to a heavy cast iron skillet to reach a depth of about ½ inch. Heat the oil to 350°, using a kitchen thermometer to check that it's reached the right heat.

11. Drain the buttermilk from the oysters. Toss drained oysters with the cracker/masa mixture until oysters are evenly coated on all sides.

12. Shake off any extra crumbs as you place the oysters in the hot skillet. Pan fry on each side for 1-2 minutes or until golden brown. Do not overcook the oysters; they should feel semi-firm but not rubbery.

13. Remove oysters from the skillet to paper towels to drain briefly.

DISH ASSEMBLY: *Warm 6 serving bowls. Ladle hot chowder into each bowl and top each serving with 3 crispy oysters. Serve immediately.*

WATERMELON GAZPACHO
Serves 4–6

This is a sumptuous shot of cool refreshing flavors that are perfect when picked from the hot summer garden. The fun part is figuring out the best way to squeeze a watermelon, as watermelons don't exactly fit in most juice presses. (Don't worry, the instructions are in the recipe.)

Ingredients:
3 cups freshly-squeezed watermelon juice
¾ cup red seedless grapes, sliced
¼ cup green onions, minced
2 tablespoons fresh cilantro, minced
1 cup tomatoes, peeled and diced
½ cup cucumber, peeled, seeded and diced
¼ cup yellow bell pepper, seeded and diced
2 tablespoons red onion, minced
1 or 2 serrano chiles, seeded and minced
1 tablespoon freshly-squeezed lime juice
Kosher salt and freshly ground black pepper

Preparation:
1. Place pieces of fresh, peeled watermelon meat in a food processor and pulse to break down the fruit to a chunky puree. Now, either transfer the puree to a fine mesh strainer and push the liquid through with a spoon to extract as much juice as possible, or use a food mill to do the job. Be sure to remove any seeds.

2. Mix the watermelon juice with the remaining ingredients. Taste and season with salt and pepper.

3. Place the mixture in the refrigerator for a few hours to allow the flavors to marry.

4. Serve in well-chilled bowls.

MARRYING FLAVORS

One of the simplest things you can do to boost flavor in many dishes is to allow flavors to marry, meld and bloom. This technique is especially helpful when you are working with a mixture of acids (tomatoes and lime juice in this recipe), aromatics (cilantro) and spices (serrano chile) as are found in most gazpachos. Allowing the mixture to rest for a few hours gives the acids time to mellow and the aromatics and spices time to bloom, producing a dish with a more complex flavor.

GO TEXAN.®

I am a big supporter of the GO TEXAN program through the Texas Department of Agriculture, which promotes Texas products, culture and communities. The program has introduced me to some of the finest ingredients I've ever worked with — from Gulf Coast shrimp, crab and snapper, to Hill Country quail and lamb, and wines that will knock your socks off. Because I insist on giving my guests the very best, I reach for GO TEXAN products first every time. They rarely disappoint.

This recipe proves that couples who cook together complement each other — at least that's true of my wife Mariana and me. I don't like cooking roux, but I have a strong passion for gumbo. Fortunately, Mariana makes a great roux, and actually enjoys it. So she does the roux, I do the gumbo and magic happens!

Ingredients:

½ cup safflower oil
½ cup all-purpose flour
1 cup yellow onions, ½-inch dice
¾ cup celery, ½-inch dice
⅓ cup fresh poblano chile, ½-inch dice
⅓ cup red bell pepper, ½-inch dice
2 tablespoons fresh jalapeño, minced
1 tablespoon fresh garlic, minced
2 bay leaves
½ teaspoon freshly ground black pepper
½ teaspoon dried thyme
½ teaspoon dried basil
½ teaspoon dried oregano
¼ teaspoon ground white pepper
6½ cups shrimp stock (or chicken stock or water)
¾ cup fresh tomatoes, diced
¾ cup Opa's Country Blend Smoked Sausage, sliced into ⅓-inch rounds
1 pound medium Texas wild-caught shrimp, peeled and deveined
1 cup cooked crawfish tail meat
Kosher salt
1 teaspoon Tabasco Sauce
¼ teaspoon cayenne pepper
2 cups cooked white rice, hot

Preparation:

1. Heat a heavy-bottomed saucepan over medium-high heat. Add oil and flour for the roux.

2. Cook flour and oil mixture, stirring continuously with a wooden spoon until the roux becomes the color of milk chocolate, about 20–25 minutes. Do not allow the roux to burn. If you begin to notice black specs in the roux or if it smokes strongly, discard it after it cools and start again.

3. Once the roux has achieved the desired color, turn the heat to low and add in the onions, celery, peppers and garlic. Stir the vegetables in the roux until they begin to soften, then stir in the bay leaf, black pepper, thyme, basil, oregano and white pepper. Allow the mixture to cook for a couple more minutes until the herbs become aromatic.

4. Turn the heat to high and begin to whisk in the stock, 1 cup at a time, until it is fully incorporated.

5. Let the gumbo come to a boil for a couple of minutes then reduce the heat to a low simmer. Add the sausage and simmer for about 1 hour, adding more stock or water if the gumbo becomes too thick.

6. Turn the heat back up to medium and add in the shrimp. Cook for about 2 minutes or until the shrimp turn pink and begin to curl. Add the crawfish tails and simmer for 1 minute more.

7. Remove the gumbo from the heat and taste it, adding salt, cayenne and Tabasco to taste.

8. Ladle hot gumbo into bowls or cups and add a scoop of hot rice into the center of each serving.

CHEF'S NOTE: *Both the roux and the sausage can leave a layer of oil floating on top of the gumbo after it has simmered for a while. Use a ladle to skim off and discard the excess oil prior to serving.*

OPA'S SMOKED MEATS

Still family operated since 1947, this Fredericksburg staple is a Hill Country classic through and through. The old world German techniques have never changed, and neither have the recipes for the fully cooked sausages and smoked meats. Opa's remains true to its roots as a smokehouse and meat locker, still hand-trimming beef and pork and slow-smoking all its products in-house. The sausages alone are so popular that Opa's sells more than 2.5 million pounds of sausage annually. I find the mixture of pork and beef in the Country Blend Smoked Sausage is ideal for gumbo. If you're visiting Fredericksburg, you can buy any of Opa's sausages and smoked meats by the pound at their market and deli in downtown Fredericksburg, and get a few sticks of jerky and a sandwich for the road. You can also order it online. Just be sure you time the delivery to get there when your gumbo roux is perfect.

VENISON BLACK BEAN CHILI
Yield: 1 gallon

Chili can't be beat as a crowd-pleasing meal—and this recipe will feed a crowd! There's always a discussion about whether or not adding beans to chili is "authentic." I like chili. I like beans, and in fact, I like beans in my chili. If you don't, that's fine. Just leave them out.

Ingredients:

3 tablespoons safflower oil
5 pounds ground venison, coarse chili grind
⅓ cup safflower oil
5 strips bacon, ¼-inch dice
2 cups yellow onions, ¼-inch dice
2 cups fresh poblanos, ¼-inch dice
¼ cup fresh jalapeños, minced
2 tablespoons fresh garlic, minced
2 medium fresh tomatoes
3 pasilla chiles
¼ cup dark chili powder
2 tablespoons ground cumin
1 tablespoon freshly ground black pepper
¼ cup all-purpose flour
¼ cup masa harina
10 cups venison, chicken or veal stock
2 cups cooked black beans
Kosher salt
Spicy Toasted Pepitas (hulled pumpkin seeds –
    see recipe page 187)
2 cups Veldhuizen Texas Gold Cheddar cheese
    (or your favorite cheddar), grated

Preparation:

1. Place 3 tablespoons of oil in a large saucepan over medium-high heat and add the venison. You may need to cook the meat in 2 batches to avoid overcrowding the pan. Brown the meat fully, then move it to a colander to drain off excess fat.

2. Bring the saucepan back up to medium heat and add remaining ⅓ cup of oil and bacon.

3. Cook the bacon, stirring frequently, until the edges begin to brown slightly.

4. Add the onions, poblanos, jalapeños and garlic and cook until the vegetables begin to turn translucent. Do not allow the vegetables to brown.

5. Meanwhile, remove the cores from the tomatoes. Place cored tomatoes on a hot grill or under a broiler. Cook until the skin begins to blacken and crack. Place the pasilla chiles on the grill with the tomatoes, allowing them to toast lightly until fragrant.

6. Remove the tomatoes and pasillas from the grill. Discard the stems and seeds from the chiles.

7. Place tomatoes and chiles in a food processor while they are still hot, and pulse until well pulverized. Reserve the mixture.

8. Add the chili powder, cumin, black pepper, flour and masa harina to the saucepan and sauté with the vegetables briefly until the mixture becomes fragrant.

9. Whisk stock into the saucepan, a little at a time to avoid creating lumps. Stir in tomato/pasilla mixture.

10. Return the cooked venison to the liquid and bring the mixture to a boil. Immediately reduce the heat and simmer for 40 minutes, stirring occasionally.

11. Add black beans and adjust the seasoning with kosher salt.

12. Garnish each serving with toasted pepitas and grated cheese.

CURRIED PHEASANT, SAUSAGE AND APPLE CHOWDER

Yield: 8 cups or 5 serving bowls

This dish was created as part of a Fredericksburg Wine Road 290 event, specifically to pair with Pedernales Cellars Viognier. It's worth mentioning that their 2012 Viognier Reserve won the prestigious Grand Gold award at the 2013 Lyon International Wine Competition, competing against wines from the French region where Viognier originated! I also like to pair this dish with Roussanne, which is gaining popularity with Texas vintners now too. With either one, you'll find the assertive curry is balanced by the bright citrus and firm acids of these wines.

Ingredients:

⅓ cup safflower oil
1 cup celery, ½-inch dice
1 cup carrots, peeled, ½-inch dice
1½ cups yellow onions, ½-inch dice
3 cloves garlic, minced
3 tablespoons madras curry powder
1 teaspoon fresh thyme
2 bay leaves
⅓ cup all-purpose flour
5 cups pheasant braising liquid, chicken stock
   or water
1½ cups russet potatoes, peeled, ¾-inch dice
1 cup heavy cream
1 cup smoked polish sausage, sliced
2 cups Oven Braised Pheasant (see recipe)
Kosher salt and freshly ground black pepper
½ cup dried apples, ¼-inch dice

Preparation:

1. Heat a heavy-bottomed soup pot over medium heat. Add oil and swirl, then add celery, carrots, onions and garlic, cooking slowly until the vegetables begin to get semi-soft and translucent.

2. Stir in curry powder, thyme and bay leaves. Allow to cook for about 3 minutes, stirring frequently until the mixture becomes very fragrant. Do not burn the spices.

3. Add flour to the pan and stir until incorporated.

4. Add the braising liquid (or combination of liquids to equal 5 total cups), 1 cup at a time, stirring well after each addition to fully incorporate the liquid.

5. Turn the heat to high and bring to a boil for 3 minutes, then reduce the heat to a simmer.

6. Add the potatoes and allow soup to simmer for about 20 minutes or until the potatoes are tender.

7. Stir in cream, sausage and pheasant and simmer for about 5 minutes more.

8. Adjust seasoning with salt and pepper.

DISH ASSEMBLY: *Place equal amounts of diced dried apple into each serving cup or bowl. Ladle hot soup over and serve immediately.*

Oven Braised Pheasant
Yield: 2 cups

Ingredients:

4 tablespoons safflower oil
2 pheasant drumsticks
2 pheasant thighs
Kosher salt and freshly ground black pepper
¼ cup yellow onions, chopped
1 medium carrot, chopped
1 celery rib, chopped
2 bay leaves
1 teaspoon fresh thyme
3 cups chicken stock or water

Preparation:

1. Preheat oven to 350°.

2. Heat oil in a small heavy-bottomed braising pan or saucepot over medium-high heat.

3. Season pheasant pieces with salt and pepper. Add to the hot pan and cook until deeply brown, about 5 minutes, then turn the pieces over and brown well on the other side.

4. Remove pheasant from the pan and set aside. Add onions, carrots and celery to the pan, browning for a few minutes.

5. Return pheasant to the pan, add herbs and chicken stock, turn heat up to high and bring the stock to a boil. As soon as it reaches a boil, remove it from the heat and cover the pan tightly with a lid or foil.

6. Place the covered pan in the center of a preheated 350° oven and allow to cook for about 50 minutes, or until the meat is tender and falling off the bone.

7. Allow the pheasant to remain in the cooking liquid until it has cooled enough to be handled. Strain and reserve the cooking liquid for use in the chowder.

8. Use your fingers to pull the pheasant meat from the bones, removing and discarding the skin and any gristle or tendons. Set finished meat aside.

BROWN VEAL STOCK AND DEMI-GLACE
Yield: 2 quarts, 2 cups demi-glace

Brown veal stock has a multitude of uses — most notably as a robust starting liquid for stews, soups, chili and braised beef or veal dishes. It is also the primary ingredient in the "king" of sauces, demi-glace. If you can't find veal bones, beef bones are an OK substitute, but the flavor of the finished stock won't be as deep. Veal bones contain more collagen, creating more gelatin for a thicker, richer stock. Brown veal stock requires more cooking time than chicken stock, but not more attention. I suggest you make both and keep them on hand.

Ingredients:
5 pounds veal soup bones
1 pound onions, peeled, cut into 2-inch pieces
¼ head celery, cut into 2-inch pieces
½ pound carrots, peeled, cut into 2-inch pieces
1 cup tomato paste
2 bay leaves
1 teaspoon fresh thyme
1 tablespoon black peppercorns

Preparation:
1. Preheat oven to 350°.

2. Place veal bones in a roasting pan and top bones with onion, celery and carrot pieces.

3. Roast for 1–2 hours or until bones and vegetables have turned dark brown but not black.

4. Remove pan from oven and spread tomato paste over bones. Return pan to oven and roast until the tomato paste browns, around 20 minutes more.

5. Allow bones and vegetables to cool, then move the mixture to a large stock pot.

6. Cover with cold water and slowly bring liquid to a simmer.

7. As the stock simmers, skim off and discard any foam that rises to the surface. Add herbs and peppercorns, bring to a full simmer and allow to cook for 8 hours, making certain it does not reach a rolling boil. Add cool water as needed to keep the level of the liquid above the bones.

8. Strain and cool the stock and remove any fat that rises to the surface. It is now ready to use.

Demi-glace
Yield: About 3 cups

Ingredients:
2 cups red wine
½ pound white/button mushrooms
2 quarts Brown Veal Stock
Kosher salt and freshly ground black pepper

Preparation:
1. Place all ingredients in a saucepan over medium heat. Skim occasionally and cook until the mixture reduces by two-thirds. Strain then season accordingly with salt and pepper.

CHICKEN STOCK
Yield: 2 quarts

There are few things in life more satisfying than the smell of chicken stock simmering on the stove. Without a doubt, stocks are one of the most quintessential ingredients used to create savory recipes. Because stock is the key ingredient in most soups and sauces, if you have a bad or weak stock, you'll produce a less-than-enticing meal. However, creating a splendid stock is not only easy, but rewarding, especially when you take proper care to produce it. Without a doubt, creating a fresh stock at home is certainly better than relying on heavily-salted commercial broths or bouillons. The taste is far richer, and your home will smell wonderful for days.

Ingredients:
4 pounds chicken bones, necks and backs
1 pound onions, peeled, cut into 1-inch pieces
2 leeks, cut into 1-inch pieces
⅓ head celery, cut into 1-inch pieces
1 bay leaf
1 teaspoon fresh thyme
1 tablespoon black peppercorns

Preparation:
1. Rinse chicken under cool water to remove any blood or impurities.

2. Place chicken and vegetables in a large stockpot. Add enough cold water to cover.

3. Bring mixture slowly to a simmer. As it begins to simmer, you'll notice an unsightly foam surfacing to the top. Use a slotted spoon to lightly skim off the foam and discard it.

4. When there is no more foam, add the herbs and peppercorns. Allow seasoned stock to cook for 4 hours at a full simmer, making certain it does not reach a rolling boil. Add cool water as needed to keep the level of the liquid above the bones.

5. Strain and cool the stock, removing any fat that rises to the surface. It is now ready to use, or can be reduced to half its volume for an even richer base stock.

CHEF'S NOTE: *You'll notice no salt was added to the stock, so it may seem to lack flavor at this point. But don't be tempted to add salt during the cooking process. Instead, wait until you have finished reducing it and are ready to use it in a recipe. Remember, stock is a building block of fine cuisine, not a finished product. You'll have nothing but "Salt Soup" if you fail to heed this warning.*

Color, texture, zest and freshness make our Cabernet Grill salads and dressings stand out in a crowd. Any one of them is a nice interim between courses, or can serve as a satisfying, light meal.

SALADS

★ ★ ★ ★ ★

★ ★ ★ ★ ★

CABERNET GRILL CAESAR SALAD
with Roasted Poblano Caesar Dressing and Homemade Croutons | Serves 4

I use this recipe at home, and once you do, you'll see why it's a family favorite. Store any remaining dressing in the refrigerator for up to 4 days, as the anchovies and egg yolks won't hold any longer than that.

Ingredients:

1 head romaine lettuce, cleaned, trimmed,
   cut into 3-inch squares
¾ cup Asiago cheese, shaved
¾ cup Roasted Poblano Caesar Dressing (see recipe)
1 cup Homemade Croutons (see recipe)

Preparation:

1. Toss all ingredients together in a large bowl.

2. Serve immediately.

Roasted Poblano Caesar Dressing
Ingredients:

3 egg yolks
1 poblano chile, roasted and peeled
1 teaspoon fresh garlic, minced
1 teaspoon Worcestershire sauce
4 anchovy filets
2 tablespoons red wine vinegar
1½ tablespoons freshly-squeezed lemon juice
2 teaspoons Dijon mustard
1½ cups virgin olive oil
½ teaspoon kosher salt
¼ teaspoon freshly ground black pepper

Preparation:

1. Place all ingredients except oil in a food processor and puree.

2. With the processor running, slowly add oil to form an emulsion. Chill until ready to use.

3. Store refrigerated and covered for up to 4 days and stir before serving.

Homemade Croutons
Yield: 3 cups

Ingredients:
3 cups day-old baguette bread
1 teaspoon Crouton Seasoning (see recipe)
¼ cup olive oil

Preparation:
1. Preheat oven to 350°.

2. Cut bread into quarters lengthwise and then slice into ½-inch thick pieces.

3. Place bread in a large bowl and toss with Crouton Seasoning and olive oil.

4. Spread bread in a single layer on a sheet pan lined with parchment paper. Bake for about 12 minutes, or until golden brown and crisp all the way through.

5. Allow to cool before tossing in the salad.

6. Store extra croutons in an airtight container for up to a week.

Crouton Seasoning
Yield: ½ cup

Ingredients:
1 tablespoon dried thyme
2 tablespoons granulated dried garlic
1½ tablespoons dried oregano
1½ tablespoons dried basil
2 tablespoons freshly ground black pepper
1½ tablespoons kosher salt

Preparation:
1. Mix all ingredients.

2. Store in an airtight container.

CHEF'S NOTE: *This mix can also be used to season roasted or grilled meats, potatoes and vegetables.*

FORMING A BOND

When you mix two liquids that would not naturally combine together, like oil and vinegar, you create an emulsion. To make a permanent emulsion like the one in this dressing (unlike a temporary emulsion in a vinaigrette), you have to start slowly to build a stronger and more enduring bond. The trick is to get the other ingredients — the emulsifiers — moving quickly and then introduce the oil drop by drop at first — in a way, getting the emulsifiers used to absorbing and bonding with the oil. Once they've accepted the first drops by evenly dispersing them, you can begin to slowly stream in the rest of the oil. Those first drops are essential in building the bond, though, so don't rush the process or you could "break" or separate the ingredients again. And you'd have to start over.

To make salads taste better, make your own dressings. We have been doing this since the day we opened the restaurant and to much applause. Commercially produced versions contain homogenizers, stabilizers and additives to make them look good—but also negatively change the taste. The following vinaigrettes are simple, healthy and better tasting than anything you'll find on a shelf, so it's well worth the extra effort.

BALSAMIC HONEY VINAIGRETTE
Yield: 2 cups

Ingredients:
1 teaspoon fresh garlic, minced
1 tablespoon shallot, minced
¼ cup red onions, ¼ inch dice
1 tablespoon fresh parsley, minced
3 tablespoons local honey
2 tablespoons Dijon mustard
1 tablespoon freshly-squeezed lemon juice
¼ cup balsamic vinegar
1 cup virgin olive oil (I do not suggest extra virgin)
2 teaspoons kosher salt
1 tablespoon freshly cracked black pepper

Preparation:
1. Place all ingredients in a medium mixing bowl, except olive oil, salt and pepper. Whisk together.

2. Add oil in a slow stream, whisking vigorously to incorporate.

3. When oil is incorporated, adjust seasoning accordingly with salt and pepper.

4. Keep refrigerated and re-whisk before using.

CHAMPAGNE VINAIGRETTE
Yield: 1¾ cups

The slightly sweet flavor of this dressing pairs well with baby spring lettuces. I like to use a colorful mix of any varieties I can find, especially baby lollo rosso, tatsoi, frisée, red oak, romaine, mizuna and radicchio.

Ingredients:
2 tablespoons shallots, minced
¼ cup Creole mustard
¼ cup local honey
2 tablespoons fresh chives (or scallion tops), minced
2 tablespoons Champagne vinegar
1 cup virgin olive oil (I do not suggest extra virgin)
Kosher salt and freshly ground black pepper

Preparation:
1. Place all ingredients in a medium mixing bowl, except oil, salt and pepper. Whisk together.

2. Add oil in a slow stream, whisking vigorously to incorporate.

3. When oil is incorporated, adjust seasoning accordingly with salt and pepper.

4. Allow dressing to sit for 2 hours at room temperature before serving.

CHEF'S NOTE: *Because this type of dressing is neither mechanically emulsified nor laden with artificial stabilizers, you will need to whisk it vigorously before each use. It is also important to note that olive oil congeals when refrigerated. If you store this dressing in the refrigerator, let it come to room temperature for at least 20 minutes before tossing it with greens.*

MANGO CHIVE VINAIGRETTE
Yield: 2½ cups

Ingredients:

1 cup ripe mangoes, peeled and sliced
¼ cup shallots, minced
1 tablespoon fresh chives, minced
1 tablespoon freshly squeezed lemon juice
2 tablespoons Champagne vinegar
¾ cup safflower oil
Kosher salt and freshly ground black pepper

Preparation:

1. Puree mango in a blender.

2. Place mango puree, shallots, chives, lemon juice and vinegar in a medium mixing bowl. Mix together.

3. Add oil in a slow stream, whisking vigorously to incorporate.

4. When oil is incorporated, adjust seasoning accordingly with salt and pepper.

5. Refrigerate for at least 4 hours and re-whisk dressing before serving.

OLIVE VINAIGRETTE
Yield: 3 cups

Ingredients:

¼ cup black olives, pitted
¼ cup green olives, pitted
1 tablespoon shallots, minced
1 teaspoon garlic, minced
1 tablespoon fresh parsley, minced
1 tablespoon green onions, minced
1 tablespoon fresh basil, minced
¼ cup peperoncini, stems removed and minced
¼ cup red wine vinegar
¼ cup Dijon mustard
1 tablespoon local honey
½ cup extra virgin olive oil
Kosher salt and freshly ground black pepper

Preparation:

1. Place all ingredients in a medium mixing bowl, except olive oil, salt and pepper. Whisk together.

2. Add oil in a slow stream, whisking vigorously to incorporate.

3. When oil is incorporated, adjust seasoning accordingly with salt and pepper.

4. Refrigerate overnight for best flavor.

5. Allow dressing to come to room temperature and re-whisk before serving.

GORGONZOLA WALNUT DRESSING
Yield: 3 cups

The secret to this recipe is warming the cheese to release the true "bleu" flavor. This is one of our most popular dressings at the Cabernet Grill. If you want to add a little bit of a Texas twist, use pecans instead of walnuts.

Ingredients:
1 cup gorgonzola cheese, crumbled, divided in half
¼ cup walnut pieces
½ cup sour cream
½ cup mayonnaise
¾ cup buttermilk
1 tablespoon Champagne vinegar
1 tablespoon fresh chives, minced
Kosher salt and freshly ground black pepper

Preparation:
1. Preheat oven to 350°.

2. Line a baking pan with foil. Spread ½ cup of gorgonzola in the pan and top the cheese with the walnut pieces.

3. Bake for about 10 minutes or until cheese starts to melt and bubble slightly. Do not allow the cheese to brown.

4. Place melted cheese, walnuts and all remaining ingredients in a bowl. Mix well.

5. Stir in reserved cheese and season with salt and pepper.

6. Refrigerate at least 4 hours before serving.

CRISPY NOODLE, ARUGULA & BEET SALAD

with Fragrant Ginger Vinaigrette | Serves 4 to 6

The growing season in Texas is longer and earlier than in many other states. This salad takes advantage of the crossover in the seasons (between spring and summer) when some of the final beets and leafy greens are being harvested and the first peppers and tomatoes are cropping up. Try roasting fresh beets, instead of boiling them, to add a deeper flavor.

Ingredients:

3 cups peanut oil
6 wonton skins, refrigerated
1 handful rice sticks
¼ cup red bell pepper, julienned
¼ cup yellow bell pepper, julienned
¼ cup cooked beets, diced small
¼ cup black beans, cooked
¼ cup wild rice, cooked
1 cup snow pea sprouts (or bean sprouts)
1 cup fresh spinach, julienned
1 cup fresh arugula, cut into bite-sized pieces
¼ cup pumpkin seeds or sliced almonds
1½ cups Fragrant Ginger Dressing (see recipe)

Preparation:

1. In a large sauce pan, heat peanut oil to 375°.

2. Stack wonton skins on a cutting board and cut into long strips about ¼-inch wide. Work quickly so the wontons do not dry out or warm up and stick together. Once cut, separate the layers by tossing lightly.

3. Drop a handful of wonton strips into the hot oil and fry for about 1 minute or until they're golden brown and crisp. Don't crowd them in the oil. Drain each batch on paper towels.

4. After the final batch of wontons, bring the oil back up to 375°. Drop some of the rice sticks into the hot oil, and allow them to puff until crispy. This happens very quickly, so watch closely. Remove and drain on paper towels, then repeat the process with the remaining rice sticks.

5. Place the remaining vegetables, beans, nuts, rice, and crispy wontons and rice sticks into a large bowl. Toss lightly with the dressing, trying not to crush the wontons and rice noodles as you toss.

Fragrant Ginger Dressing
Yield: 1½ cups

Ingredients:

2 tablespoons fresh ginger root, peeled and minced
1 tablespoon Sambal Oelek
3 scallions, minced
1 tablespoon fresh mint, minced
1 tablespoon fresh basil, minced
1 tablespoon fresh cilantro, minced
¼ cup freshly-squeezed lime juice
¼ cup freshly-squeezed grapefruit juice
¼ cup safflower oil
¼ cup brown sugar

Preparation:

1. Whisk together all ingredients in a small bowl.

2. Dressing can be refrigerated for up to 3 days, and re-whisked before using.

CUCUMBER & SMOKED PEPPER CREMA SALAD

with Grilled Texas Wild-Caught Shrimp | Serves 4

I developed this dish for a vintner dinner with Grape Creek Vineyards, and paired it with their Pinot Grigio. The smokiness of the peppers matched well with the oak tones from the wine's aging barrels, while the bright crispness and acidity of the wine cut the richness of both the shrimp and sour cream. The flavors blended harmoniously and we got rave reviews. Try serving it the same way, with Pinot Grigio, and see if you don't get rave reviews too.

Ingredients:

2 small red bell peppers
½ pound medium size Texas wild-caught shrimp, peeled and deveined
1 teaspoon Cabernet Grill Cajun Seasoning
1 tablespoon safflower oil
1 English cucumber, cut in half lengthwise and sliced ⅛-inch thick, to make 3 cups
⅓ cup red onions, cut into a very thin julienne
1 tablespoon shallots, minced
1 clove garlic, minced
½ cup sour cream
2 tablespoons mayonnaise
1 tablespoon fresh dill, minced
1 teaspoon granulated sugar
Kosher salt and freshly ground black pepper

Preparation:

1. Prepare a gas or charcoal grill and bring the heat to high.

2. Place the red peppers on the grill and blacken on all sides to blister the skin. When blistered, move peppers to a kitchen towel, wrap them up well, and allow them to steam a bit and cool in the towel.

3. Season shrimp with Cabernet Grill Cajun Seasoning, then brush them with a little oil and place them on the grill. Cook for 2–3 minutes on each side until the shrimp turns pink and starts to curl a bit and the center of the shrimp turns opaque. Do not overcook. Remove the shrimp from the grill and allow to cool.

4. Set a smoker to cold smoke with either oak or hickory wood, according to manufactures directions.

5. Peel away the charred skin from the red peppers and remove seeds.

6. Place the peppers in the smoker for about 20 minutes or until they pick up a good smoke flavor. Remove the peppers from the smoker and cut them into julienne strips about ¼-inch wide and 2 inches long.

7. Place the peppers in a bowl. Add shrimp and remaining ingredients and toss altogether well. Adjust seasoning accordingly with salt and pepper.

8. Chill in the refrigerator before serving.

9. Serve as is, or place a heaping spoonful on a bed of arugula or Mesclun greens.

GINGER MANGO CARROT SLAW
Yield: 2 cups/Serves 6–8

The secret to this slaw is finding mangos that are not soft and ripe, but also not hard as a rock. Look for very firm fruit that is yellow inside. This pungent slaw is great on pulled pork sandwiches, in fish tacos or as an accompaniment to most anything fried.

Ingredients:
¼ cup freshly-squeezed lime juice
1 tablespoon fresh ginger root, peeled and minced
⅓ cup light brown sugar
2 tablespoons shallots, minced
2 tablespoons safflower oil
2 cups carrots, peeled and shredded
1½ cups unripe mango, peeled and shredded
1 teaspoon Sriracha Sauce
Kosher salt and freshly ground black pepper

Preparation:
1. Mix all ingredients together in medium-size bowl and adjust seasoning accordingly with salt and pepper.

2. Cover and refrigerate for 1 hour.

3. Stir before serving.

HATCH CHILE CORNBREAD SALAD
Yield: Enough for a potluck supper

This is an ideal dish to take to a potluck because it's flavorful and will last for hours on a table, getting better as the flavors meld. Yes, it's truly one ugly looking salad, but the taste is beautiful! The best thing about taking it to a potluck? Because it's not pretty, folks will pass it by. That means there's enough for you to take back home and enjoy. If they had only known...

Ingredients:

1⅓ cup mayonnaise
2 tablespoons freshly-squeezed lemon juice
1 clove garlic, minced
1 teaspoon crushed red pepper (optional)
½ teaspoon freshly ground black pepper
5 strips crisp-cooked bacon, ½-inch dice
4 cups day-old cornbread, crumbled
    into 1-inch pieces
½ cup Hatch chiles, roasted peeled and
    seeded, minced
½ cup sweet corn kernels, cooked
1 cup vine ripe tomatoes, diced into ½-inch pieces
1 avocado, peeled, pitted and diced ½-inch pieces
⅓ cup red bell pepper, ¼-inch dice
2 hard-boiled eggs, peeled and chopped
Kosher salt

Preparation:

1. In a small bowl, whisk together mayonnaise, lemon juice, garlic and peppers.

2. Place remaining ingredients into a medium-size bowl. Fold in mayo mixture. Check seasoning and add salt if needed.

3. Refrigerate for at least an hour before serving.

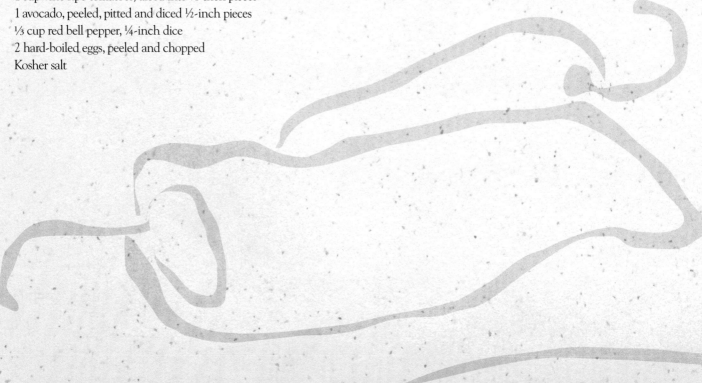

TWO PIG SALAD
with Warm Two Pig Dressing | Serves 4–6

I have always loved spinach salad with warm bacon dressing. Adding Tasso ham just takes it to a new level. This dish proves my three Bs rule: Adding butter, bacon or bourbon simply makes things taste better. I can tell you from experience, even people who say they hate salad will ask for a second serving of this one. (You probably don't want to visit your cardiologist the day after eating this, but then again, maybe you should!)

Ingredients:
1 tablespoon safflower oil
1 clove garlic, minced
1 cup baby portabella mushrooms
   (aka crimini mushrooms), sliced
4 handfuls baby spinach, cleaned
½ cup gorgonzola cheese, crumbled
Warm Two Pig Dressing (see recipe)
Freshly ground black pepper

Preparation:
1. Heat a small skillet over medium-high heat and add oil. Add garlic and mushrooms; sauté until mushrooms are lightly browned on the edges and pliable. Remove the pan from the heat.

2. Place spinach in a medium bowl and toss with mushroom sauté, cheese and Warm Two Pig Dressing.

3. Top with a few grinds from a peppermill and serve immediately.

Warm Two Pig Dressing
Yield: 1 cup

Ingredients:
1 tablespoon safflower oil
2 strips applewood smoked bacon, ¼-inch dice
¼ cup Tasso ham, ¼-inch dice
¼ cup red onions, ¼-inch dice
1 pinch teaspoon freshly ground black pepper
2 tablespoons Creole mustard
2 tablespoons brown sugar
1 tablespoon balsamic vinegar
1 teaspoon Worcestershire sauce
¼ cup safflower oil

Preparation:
1. In a small sauce pan over medium heat, add the safflower oil and the bacon.

2. Stir bacon occasionally until it is mostly rendered and the edges begin to brown.

3. Add the Tasso ham and onions, continuing to stir occasionally. Cook until the onions are translucent and the ham and bacon are caramelized.

4. Stir in the pepper, mustard, brown sugar, vinegar and Worcestershire, allowing the mixture to bubble a bit.

5. Remove pan from the heat and whisk in the olive oil.

6. Taste: The bacon and ham should provide enough salt, but you can check to see if you want more and add it sparingly.

7. Serve warm and well-whisked before tossing with the salad mixture.

Our entrées bring us rave reviews, and now they can bring you the same acclaim. Follow this simple recipe for creating your own signature dishes at home: Whenever possible, source your ingredients from the bounty of Texas farms, ranches, fields, streams and the Gulf Coast, then take time to build the flavors. Stand back and accept the praise.

ENTREES

★ ★ ★ ★ ★

★ ★ ★ ★ ★

ALMOND CORNFLAKE CRUSTED CATFISH
with Mango Chutney Mayo and Texas Citrus Slaw | Serves 4

Over the years, this recipe has been passed (or stolen) from one chef to another, condensed and tweaked every time. As best as I can tell, it may have started out as "Hot & Crunchy Trout with Mango Aioli" created by Chef Jeff Blank at Hudson's on the Bend in Austin. My version of the dish has been a good earner for years. So all I can say is, thanks, Jeff. I owe you one!

Ingredients:

1½ cups unsweetened cornflakes
½ cup + 1 tablespoon almond slices, toasted
½ teaspoon crushed red pepper
2 pounds catfish fillets, boneless/skinless
1 teaspoon Cabernet Grill Cajun Seasoning
¼ cup unsalted butter, melted
¾ cup Mango Chutney Mayo (see recipe)
1 tablespoon fresh cilantro, minced

Mango Chutney Mayo | Yield: 1 cup

Ingredients:

¾ cup mayonnaise
3 tablespoons Major Grey's Mango Chutney (any brand)
2 teaspoons Sriracha Sauce

Preparation:

Place all ingredients in a small food processor and puree. Keep refrigerated.

Preparation:

1. Preheat oven to 350°.

2. Place cornflakes and ½ cup of almonds in a food processor and pulse until the mixture is finely ground. Stir in the red pepper.

3. Dry off the catfish filets with a paper towel to remove any excess moisture, but do not dry them completely.

4. Season fish filets with Cabernet Grill Cajun Seasoning.

5. Place the cornflake mixture on a platter and press the catfish filets into the cornflakes to coat each filet evenly on both sides. Shake off any excess coating.

6. Heat a large skillet over medium-high heat, add the melted butter, and lay the catfish filets in the pan in a single layer. Be careful not to overcrowd the pan. Cook filets for about 1½–3 minutes on each side until golden brown.

7. Transfer browned filets to a sheet pan and place in the oven for 15–17 minutes, or until the fish is golden brown and flakes easily when pressed with a fork.

Texas Citrus Slaw | Yield: 3½ cups

You'll probably find yourself reaching for this recipe time and again. Try it in fish tacos or alongside fried shrimp and oysters.

Ingredients:

¼ cup safflower oil
¼ cup granulated sugar
1 teaspoon minced orange zest
¼ cup freshly-squeezed Texas Ruby Red grapefruit juice
1 tablespoon fresh ginger root, minced
2 tablespoons fresh cilantro, minced
1 cup red cabbage, shredded
1 cup carrots, shredded
½ small red bell pepper, julienned
½ small yellow bell pepper, julienned
½ cup bean sprouts (optional)
1 tablespoon fresh jalapeño, minced
½ cup Texas Ruby Red grapefruit segments
½ cup Texas Rio Grande Valley orange segments
Kosher salt and freshly ground black pepper

Preparation:

Mix all ingredients in a medium size bowl and adjust seasoning with salt and pepper.

DISH ASSEMBLY: *Place 1 or 2 filets on each plate and drizzle with the Mango Chutney Mayo. Top with the reserved tablespoon of toasted almonds and the cilantro. Serve with Texas Citrus Slaw on the side.*

TRULY TENDER RIBS

Nothing kills a day of barbecuing like tough ribs. But remember, tenderness is in your control. First of all, don't buy too big of a rack: Stick to small, 1½–1¾ pound racks. Then, be sure they are peeled — or stripped of their "silverskin." This white, opaque connective membrane is as chewy as rubber. Ask your butcher to remove it before you leave the meat counter. If you get your ribs home and see this shiny layer on the back (the curvy side with the least amount of meat), it's easy enough to remove. Use your fingernail or a knife to dig into the membrane directly at the top of an end bone. Then once you have a corner separated, use a small damp towel to get a good grip on it and pull it away from the ribs. It will usually pull off in one piece. It takes practice to get it right, but the results are worth it.

And how do you know when the ribs should be pulled from the fire? The easiest way is to simply put a pair of tongs in the middle of the rack as it rests on the grill (or in the pan). Now try to fold the ribs over in half. If they easily pull apart to fold in the middle, they're done. If the rack feels like it has a steel spring in it, keep cooking. Low and slow wins the race.

FIVE TIMES IN THE FIRE BABY BACK RIBS

with Bayou Barbecue Sauce, Citrus Pickled Spanish Onions & Roasted Potato Salad | Serves 4–6

If I could stake any claim of distinction from my culinary contribution at a legendary Burtwell family reunion, it would certainly be for the baby back ribs I served—ribs that will live in infamy. Their fame is not due to their awesome balance of sweet and spicy flavor, nor their succulent tenderness or mouth-watering appearance.

Unfortunately, those attributes will forever be overshadowed by the tragic fact that we dropped each and every rack of ribs directly into the fire pit at least 5 times. You could blame this unfortunate incident on a poor set of barbecue tongs. Or you could determine that the barbecue grill itself was inadequate for the job. You could even surmise that the quantity of beer we consumed during the event hindered our ability to successfully maneuver the ribs effectively.

Personally, I believe it was destiny! These ribs had a calling beyond our control. One after the other they dove in the fire. Then one after the other, we lifted them from the fire like a phoenix. Call it divine intervention if you will, but I truly believe these ribs tasted as if they were sent from heaven. I don't recommend you toss them into the fire. But if they fall in on their own, consider yourself blessed.

Ingredients:
2 racks baby back pork ribs (1½–1¾ pounds each)
½ cup Rib Rub (see recipe)
1 cup Rib Glaze (see recipe)

Preparation:
1. Peel membrane from the backside of ribs, or ask your butcher to do it for you. (See page 97 on how to prep ribs.)

2. Rub about ¼ cup of Rib Rub onto both sides of each rack.

3. Either roast ribs on a sheet pan in a 350° oven, or place in a smoker at 225°. Cook ribs until the meat starts to pull back from the end of the bones about ¼ to ½ inch, between 1½ and 3 hours.

4. Transfer ribs to barbecue grill over medium heat. Baste with Rib Glaze, using a pastry brush. Turn each rack 3 times, basting both sides until ribs begin to have a somewhat shiny and sticky appearance.

5. Cut ribs between bones.

CHEF'S NOTE: *Do not allow the heat to get too high or the honey in the glaze will burn.*

Rib Rub
Yield: About 1 cup

Ingredients:
2 tablespoons kosher salt
2 tablespoons granulated sugar
2 tablespoons brown sugar
2 tablespoons ground cumin
2 tablespoons coarse ground black pepper
4 tablespoons paprika
2 tablespoons chili powder
2 tablespoons granulated garlic powder
1 teaspoon cayenne pepper (optional)

Preparation:
Mix all ingredients in a small bowl until thoroughly combined. Store in an airtight container.

Rib Glaze
Yield: 1 cup

Ingredients:
½ cup local honey
½ cup balsamic vinegar

Preparation:
Whisk ingredients together in a small bowl.

Bayou Barbecue Sauce
Yield: 1½ cups

Ingredients:
¼ cup Original Louisiana Hot Sauce
1 tablespoon Worcestershire sauce
¼ cup local honey
¾ cup ketchup
2 tablespoons molasses
2 tablespoons Zatarain's Creole Mustard
2 cloves garlic, minced
1 teaspoon Cabernet Grill Cajun Seasoning

Preparation:
Mix all ingredients together. Use immediately or refrigerate sauce for up to 2 weeks.

Citrus Pickled Spanish Onions
Yield: 3 cups

A pungent, citrusy blend that counterbalances the sweetness of the ribs. Also great piled on barbecue brisket sandwiches.

Ingredients:
2 Spanish red onions (about 10 ounces each)
1 medium size orange
½ cup freshly-squeezed grapefruit juice
¼ cup red wine vinegar
¼ cup granulated sugar
1 pinch dried oregano
1 teaspoon kosher salt
1 teaspoon freshly ground black pepper

Preparation:
1. Trim ends from both onions and peel off skin. Slice onions into thin rings. Place in a medium-sized bowl.

2. Zest the rind of the orange with a micro-plane, then juice the orange. Add zest and juice to onions.

3. Add remaining ingredients and toss together well. Place the mixture into a Ziploc bag for 24 hours, turning the bag a few times.

4. Store onions in a glass container in the refrigerator and use within 3 days.

Roasted Potato Salad
Serves 8

This may be the oddest-looking potato salad you've seen. The potatoes are roasted and not boiled, so the finished salad has an uncommon dark color. However, it is precisely the roasting process that adds a deeper dimension to the flavor and raises this above other potato salads. It is a Cabernet Grill guest favorite, and I receive more recipe requests for this particular salad than for any other menu item.

Ingredients:
3 pounds red new potatoes, cut in quarters
¼ cup safflower oil
1 tablespoon Cabernet Grill Cajun Seasoning
1 tablespoon fresh parsley, minced
⅓ cup celery, diced
3 green onions, minced
⅓ cup fresh Hatch green chile, diced
⅓ cup red bell pepper, diced
⅓ cup dill pickle, diced
¼ cup Dijon mustard
2 hard-boiled eggs, peeled and chopped
1 cup mayonnaise
Kosher salt and freshly ground black pepper

Preparation:
1. Preheat oven to 350°.

2. In a medium-sized bowl, toss potatoes with oil and Cabernet Grill Cajun Seasoning.

3. Lay potatoes in a single layer on a baking sheet. Roast for 30–45 minutes, or until golden brown and tender. Allow potatoes to cool about 30 minutes.

4. In a large bowl, mix potatoes with remaining ingredients. Adjust seasoning with salt and pepper and refrigerate until ready to serve.

DISH ASSEMBLY: *Mound ribs on a platter, with or without a topping of Bayou Barbecue Sauce. Serve Roasted Potato Salad and Citrus Pickled Spanish onions in separate bowls, and the Bayou Barbecue Sauce in a gravy boat. Be sure there are plenty of napkins too!*

BACON-WRAPPED JALAPEÑO-STUFFED QUAIL

with Rosemary-Raspberry Sauce and Maple-Chipotle Sweet Potato Mash | Serves 6

Quail is a menu item that defines Texas Hill Country dining. The tender meat has a mild flavor without the gaminess of larger wild fowl. It's become so popular that it's being farmed throughout South Texas, and still has a strong hunting tradition from October to February. Unless you've harvested your own, you can usually find it in the frozen section of a grocery meat department, already semi-boneless with the tiny ribs removed.

Ingredients:

12 semi-boneless Texas quails
6 small fresh jalapeños, cut in half lengthwise
12 strips applewood smoked bacon
Kosher salt and freshly ground black pepper
Maple Chipotle Sweet Potato Mash (see recipe)
2 cups Rosemary-Raspberry Sauce, warm (see recipe)
Rosemary sprigs

Preparation:

1. Stuff each quail with a jalapeño half. Wrap quail with a slice of bacon, securing it to the bird with a toothpick.

2. Prepare a grill with mesquite wood, and bring it to medium-high heat. Lightly oil the cooking grate.

3. Season quail with salt and pepper, place it on the grill, and cook for about 5 minutes on each side, until the juices from inside the quail run clear and the bacon begins to crisp up a bit.

4. Remove toothpicks from the quail before assembling the plates.

Rosemary-Raspberry Sauce

Yield: 2 cups

Ingredients:

2 tablespoons unsalted butter or safflower oil
2 small shallots, minced
2 teaspoons fresh rosemary, minced
1 cup Veal Demi-Glace (recipe page 76)
1 cup Fischer & Wieser Raspberry Chipotle Sauce
Kosher salt and freshly ground black pepper

Preparation:

1. Heat a small saucepan over medium heat and add butter, shallots and rosemary.

2. Cook shallots lightly until they begin to turn translucent. Do not allow them to brown.

3. Stir in demi-glace and Fischer & Wieser Raspberry Chipotle Sauce, stirring gently as you heat the mixture through. Adjust seasoning with salt and pepper.

Maple-Chipotle Sweet Potato Mash
Serves 6

Ingredients:

3 pounds sweet potatoes, peeled and cubed
6 tablespoons unsalted butter
¼ cup pure maple syrup
1 tablespoon canned chipotles in adobo, minced
Kosher salt and white pepper

Preparation:

1. Place sweet potatoes in a large saucepan with enough water to cover them. Boil until tender, about 20–30 minutes, then drain completely in a colander.

2. Place drained sweet potatoes in a medium-sized bowl while still hot. Mash in butter, syrup and chipotle.

3. Adjust seasoning with salt and white pepper.

DISH ASSEMBLY: *Place a generous spoonful of Maple-Chipotle Sweet Potato Mash in the center of each serving plate. Make a shallow well in the center of the mashers. Stack 2 quails in the well. Top birds with a drizzle of Rosemary-Raspberry Sauce; garnish with rosemary sprigs.*

Fischer & Wieser of Fredericksburg

I don't often use prepackaged sauces, but Fischer & Wieser's Original Roasted Raspberry Chipotle Sauce product is so good, I make it an exception. This sauce put the local company on the culinary map in 1997, catapulting them into their standing as #1 gourmet food company in Texas. They now have more than 70 products — jams, jellies, pasta sauces, salsas, snacks — on store shelves around the country. When you stay at the Cotton Gin Village, go down the road to Das Peach Haus (Wieser's original family fruit stand) for some samples, or visit the big Fischer & Wieser store on Main Street for an even bigger choice.

IF YOU CAN'T TAKE THE HEAT

It's hard to tell which chiles are going to be super hot and which aren't—and just looking at them doesn't help. So if you want to moderate the bite a bit, and still allow the fruitiness of the pepper to shine through, simply scrape out the seeds and membrane from the cavity of the chile. If you're particularly sensitive, wear thin rubber gloves when you work with hot peppers and you won't feel the burn on your fingers either.

CAJUN PAN-SEARED SNAPPER
Topped with Lump Crab Lemon Cream Sauce and Firecracker Rice | Serves 4

The firm texture and sweetness of red snapper matches well with the spicy accents in this dish. There is now a limit on the amount of red snapper that can be commercially or recreationally fished from the Gulf of Mexico, so the price has risen over the years. But from July through September, when the fish are generally larger, the price stabilizes a bit, and that's when you should plan to make this dish at home.

Ingredients:

2 pounds red snapper filets, bones and skin removed
1 tablespoon Cabernet Grill Cajun Seasoning
½ teaspoon cayenne pepper
½ cup all-purpose flour
2 tablespoons safflower oil
2 tablespoons unsalted butter
1 cup Lemon Cream Sauce (see recipe)
6–8 ounces jumbo lump crab meat
2 green onions, minced

Preparation:

1. Preheat oven to 400°.

2. Place the fish filets on a tray in a single layer and blot with paper towels to remove excess moisture.

3. In a small bowl, mix the Cabernet Grill Seasoning and cayenne pepper. Sprinkle mixture evenly on both sides of the fish.

4. Place the flour in a medium-sized bowl. Dip each fish filet in the flour, evenly coating each side. Shake off any excess flour.

5. Pick a skillet big enough to hold all of the fish in a single layer without overcrowding, or use 2 skillets. Place skillet on medium-high heat. Add the oil and butter; heat until bubbling. Gently place the snapper in the pan and allow it to sear for 1–2 minutes on one side, until it turns just a bit golden. Flip the fish to the other side, then immediately place the skillet in the preheated oven.

6. Cook 5–8 minutes, depending on the thickness of the fish filets. The fish will be done when the filets flake easily and still look moist when you press on them. If they look dry, go back to the store and get more fish and repeat all the preceding steps.

Lemon Cream Sauce
Yield: About 1 cup

Ingredients:

1 tablespoon unsalted butter
1 shallot, sliced
¼ cup white wine
2 tablespoons freshly squeezed lemon juice
1 teaspoon Tabasco Sauce
½ bay leaf
1 small pinch fresh thyme
1½ cups heavy cream
1 teaspoon fresh lemon zest
Kosher salt

Preparation:

1. Melt butter in a small saucepan over medium-low heat. Add shallots, cooking very slowly, stirring occasionally, until they become translucent. Do not allow them to brown.

2. Increase the heat to medium and stir in the wine, lemon juice, Tabasco, bay leaf and thyme. Allow the liquid to reduce by about 75%, or until the pan is nearly dry.

3. Add the heavy cream and stir occasionally, allowing the liquid to reduce by 25% or until the sauce starts to thicken enough to lightly coat the back of a spoon. Remove from the heat and strain out the shallots and herbs.

4. Stir in the lemon zest and season with salt.

CHEF'S NOTE: *The sauce can be refrigerated for up to 5 days.*

Firecracker Rice

Serves 4–6

Ingredients:

1 tablespoon safflower oil
½ cup red onions, minced
½ cup celery, minced
1 cup Texmati long grain white rice, uncooked
1¾ cups chicken stock, boiling
¼ teaspoon fresh thyme
1 bay leaf
1 tablespoon yellow bell pepper, brunoise cut
1 tablespoon red bell pepper, brunoise cut
1 tablespoon poblano chile, brunoise cut
1 tablespoon fresh jalapeño, seeds removed,
    brunoise cut
2 tablespoons dried papaya, brunoise cut
1 pinch cayenne pepper
Kosher salt and freshly ground black pepper

Preparation:

1. Add oil to a medium-sized saucepan over medium heat. Stir in the onions and celery and sauté until the vegetables become softened and the onions are translucent. Do not allow them to brown. Add rice to the pan and stir for 1 minute.

2. Pour the boiling chicken stock into the saucepan, and stir in the thyme and bay leaf.

3. Bring the mixture back to a boil over high heat, then immediately reduce the heat to a simmer and cover tightly for 15 minutes. Remove the saucepan from the heat and allow rice to rest, covered, for 6 minutes.

4. Stir in the peppers, papaya and cayenne. Adjust seasoning with salt and pepper. Remove bay leaf and serve hot.

DISH ASSEMBLY: *While the fish is cooking, heat 1 cup of Lemon Cream Sauce in a small saucepan. Add lump crab meat and simmer for a couple of minutes until just heated through.*
To serve: *Top the fish filets with Lemon Cream/Crab Sauce. Garnish with minced green onions and a small sprinkle of Cabernet Grill Cajun Seasoning. Serve beside Firecracker Rice.*

BRUNOISE CUT

Pronounced "broon-wahz," this French culinary term defines the size and shape of the item being cut. You don't need to get a ruler out, but a "correct" brunoise cut is an ⅛-inch cube. You just need to know it's a very small, uniform dice. The small size is important in this recipe because the vegetables are mixed with grains of rice, and neither should overpower the other.

10-SECOND PEPPER PREP

1

Cut off the top and bottom of the pepper.

2

Make 1 cut to open it flat onto the board. Use your palm to flatten the pepper, loosening the seeds.

3

Run your knife along the flesh to remove the membrane and seeds in one motion.

4

The pepper is ready to be cut into even strips for uniform dices.

ALMOND DUCK SCHNITZEL

with Apple-Thyme Amaretto Sauce and Amish Butter Whipped Potatoes | Serves 4

Although including a schnitzel recipe serves as my homage to Fredericksburg's German settlers, it is the apples that anchor the dish to the Texas Hill Country. Sure, apples may not be the first fruit you associate with the region, yet the old apple orchards in Mason, just 40 miles northwest of Fredericksburg, still produce Red Delicious, Cameo, Gold Rush and Pink Ladies that locals love. Even winemakers are embracing Texas apples: Don Pullum, one of the state's finest winemakers, has developed a fantastic Cider Dessert Wine for Sandstone Winery in Mason. Pullum and Sandstone proprietors Scott Haupert and Manny Silerio have partnered on all of their amazing red blends over the years, so this apple-based wine was a natural progression for the trio. Using Texas apples for the cider base, then fortifying it with brandy, it's "as close to being Port as you can get with apples," they tell me. A glass or two is a fitting finish to this meal.

Ingredients:

6 duck breast halves (about 5 ounces each)
Kosher salt and freshly ground black pepper
½ cup sliced almonds, chopped
1½ cups fresh/soft breadcrumbs
2 teaspoons fresh chives, minced
2 tablespoons unsalted butter
2 tablespoons safflower oil
1 cup Apple-Thyme Amaretto Sauce (see recipe)

Preparation:

1. Remove the skin from the duck breasts and reserve for another use.

2. Cut the duck breasts in half. Place a few pieces of duck into a 1-gallon Ziploc bag, keeping them flat in one layer. Without sealing the bag, beat the duck medallions with a meat mallet until they are about ⅛-inch thick. Repeat until all the medallions have been flattened.

3. Season the duck lightly with salt and pepper.

4. Mix almonds, breadcrumbs and chives in a medium size bowl.

5. Put some of the breadcrumb mixture on a flat plate. Press a duck medallion into the breadcrumbs to coat evenly, turn over and repeat. Continue until all the pieces of duck are well coated.

6. Heat a large skillet over medium-high heat and add half of the safflower oil and butter. As soon as the butter begins to sizzle and starts to turn a little brown on the edges, add a single layer of the duck medallions to the pan. Cook for about 1 minute per side. The duck should be a golden brown on the outside and medium-rare to medium on the inside.

7. When cooked, remove the duck from the pan and transfer to a warm platter. Repeat, using the remaining oil and butter as needed, until all the duck medallions are cooked and arranged on the platter.

Apple-Thyme Amaretto Sauce

Yield: About 1 cup

Ingredients:

1 shallot, minced
1 tablespoon safflower oil
¼ cup Amaretto liqueur
1 cup apple cider
¼ cup apple cider vinegar
½ teaspoon fresh thyme
¼ teaspoon freshly ground black pepper
¼ cup brown sugar
1 small Granny Smith apple, peeled and diced
½ cup heavy cream
2 tablespoons unsalted butter
Kosher salt

Preparation:

1. Heat oil in a saucepan over medium heat and sweat shallots slowly until translucent.

2. Add Amaretto and allow alcohol to burn off.

3. Add cider, vinegar, thyme, pepper and brown sugar. Bring mixture to a boil and reduce volume by half.

4. Add apples to reduced liquid. Allow to simmer for 5 minutes or until apples are tender.

5. Add cream and bring mixture back to a simmer.

6. Add butter and puree mixture, using a food processor or immersion blender.

7. Adjust seasoning with salt.

Amish Butter Whipped Potatoes

Serves 6

Ingredients:

1½ pounds Yukon Gold potatoes, peeled
3 cups chicken stock or water
6 tablespoons Amish butter
½ cup heavy cream
Kosher salt and freshly ground black pepper

Preparation:

1. Cut potatoes into 3-inch chunks and place in a medium saucepan. Cover with stock or water and bring to a boil over high heat.

2. Reduce heat to medium-high and cook, uncovered, for 45 minutes or until the potatoes are fork-tender. Add more liquid if needed during cooking to keep the potatoes submerged.

3. Pour the potatoes into a colander to drain. Allow them to remain in the colander for just a couple of minutes, so the heat inside the potatoes dries them a bit.

4. While still hot, transfer the potatoes to the bowl of a standing electric mixer fitted with the whip attachment. Add the butter and heavy cream. Whip the potatoes for a couple of minutes until fairly smooth. Do not over-whip or the potatoes will become gummy.

5. Adjust seasoning with salt and pepper. Serve hot.

DISH ASSEMBLY: *Place a dollop of Amish Butter Whipped Potatoes on each plate and lean a few Almond Duck Schnitzel medallions against the potatoes. Spoon Apple-Thyme Amaretto Sauce over the duck and the potatoes and serve immediately.*

FREDERICKSBURG'S AMISH MARKET

Like many chefs, I take butter seriously. The first time I visited the Amish Market on Main Street in Fredericksburg, the "salt-of-the-earth" owners Mike and Mary Monahan introduced me to some of the best butter I've ever had—Amish Rolled Butter. I was hooked. Using old-world techniques, Amish dairies use only the cream from the top of the milk and add a tiny bit of salt to their butter, but never add whey or chemicals. The Amish Market is filled with high quality crafts, solid wood furniture, and a host of organic cheeses and home-canned goods, handmade in Amish and Mennonite communities. I hope you'll visit them when you're here in Fredericksburg.

CAJUN EGGPLANT PIROGUE STUFFED WITH BLUE CRAB AND SHRIMP AU GRATIN

with Grilled Asparagus and Blood Orange Vinaigrette | Serves 2

This is the one menu item that remains from the original menu, back when the restaurant was named the Cotton Gin Seafood and Steak Kitchen. This is a fairly traditional Cajun recipe and makes the most of mild eggplant combined with fresh Texas Gulf seafood. It's one of those menu items that returning guests will order every time they visit the restaurant.

Ingredients:

1 8-inch eggplant, cap removed, peeled
Seasoned Flour (see recipe)
Egg Wash (see recipe)
Dry breadcrumbs
1 tablespoon safflower oil
1 teaspoon garlic, minced
8 large Texas wild-caught shrimp, peeled and deveined
Kosher salt and freshly ground black pepper
1 tablespoon white wine
1 teaspoon freshly-squeezed lemon juice
½ cup lump crab meat
¾ cup Shallot Cream Sauce (see recipe)
¼ cup Asiago cheese, grated
1 tablespoon dry breadcrumbs

Preparation:

1. Preheat deep fryer to 350°.

2. Cut eggplant in half lengthwise and use a spoon to scoop out the pulp, leaving ¾-inch "walls" on the perimeter of the boat. Place hollowed eggplant in seasoned flour and shake off excess. Dip in egg wash to coat all surfaces; drain excess liquid. Evenly coat eggplant in breadcrumbs and shake off excess coating.

3. Fry until golden brown and crispy, about 4 minutes. Drain with cavity facing down on a wire rack.

4. Meanwhile, heat a small sauté pan over medium-high heat. Add oil and sauté garlic and shrimp with salt and pepper until the shrimp begin to curl slightly. Add white wine and lemon juice and stir to combine.

5. Add crab meat and Shallot Cream Sauce, heating the mixture for a couple of minutes until bubbly.

6. Pour mixture into fried eggplant boat.

7. Top with cheese and breadcrumbs; place under broiler until lightly golden and bubbly. Serve immediately.

CHEF'S NOTE: *If you plan to broil and serve the pirogue on flat surfaces (instead of in a rarebit dish with sides, like we do at the Cabernet Grill), you may need to cut a thin slice off the curved bottom before you fry it so the eggplant doesn't roll.*

Seasoned Flour
Yield: 1 cup

Ingredients:
1 cup all-purpose flour
1 tablespoon Cabernet Grill
   Cajun Seasoning

Preparation:
Mix ingredients in a medium-sized bowl.

Egg Wash
Yield: 1 cup

Ingredients:
1 cup milk
1 egg

Preparation:
Beat egg and milk together in medium-sized bowl.

Shallot Cream Sauce
Yield: About 2 cups

Ingredients:
½ cup shallots, minced
2 tablespoons safflower oil
½ cup white wine
2 cups heavy cream
½ teaspoon Tabasco Sauce
Kosher salt and freshly ground black pepper

Preparation:

1. Add shallots and oil to a small heavy-bottomed saucepan on medium-low heat.

2. Sweat the shallots until translucent, stirring often. Do not allow shallots to brown.

3. Add white wine and increase heat to medium-high.

4. Allow wine and shallot mixture to reduce by 80%.

5. Add heavy cream and reduce mixture by 25%.

6. Remove pan from heat and pour sauce through a strainer to remove shallots.

7. Place sauce back in the saucepan over low heat and add Tabasco. Whisk mixture together to incorporate; adjust seasoning with salt and pepper.

Grilled Asparagus and Red Peppers with Blood Orange Vinaigrette
Serves 4

Ingredients:
2 tablespoons freshly-squeezed blood orange juice
½ teaspoon grated blood orange zest
2 tablespoons Champagne vinegar
½ shallot, minced
½ cup extra virgin olive oil
1 teaspoon toasted sesame oil
1 tablespoon safflower oil
1 pound fresh asparagus spears
1 large red bell pepper
Kosher salt and freshly ground black pepper

Preparation:
1. Heat a charbroil grill to medium-high heat.

2. Place the orange juice, zest, vinegar and shallots in a small bowl. Using a wire whisk, whip in the olive oil in a slow steady stream until fully incorporated. Whisk in sesame oil in the same way. Adjust seasoning with salt and pepper. Set the vinaigrette aside so the flavors can marry.

3. Place asparagus and red bell pepper in a medium-sized bowl; drizzle with safflower oil and toss to coat all surfaces evenly.

4. Grill the pepper until it is blackened, with blistered skin on all sides. Remove it from the grill and wrap it in a kitchen towel to steam for about 3 minutes. Peel away and discard the blistered skin; remove the core and seeds. Do not rinse the pepper under running water.

5. Cut the pepper into julienne strips.

6. Grill the asparagus for 3–4 minutes, until lightly charred and somewhat softened.

7. Combine the asparagus and red pepper strips in a bowl and toss with the Blood Orange Vinaigrette.

THE CAJUN PIROGUE

Straight from the marshes of Louisiana, just across the Gulf of Mexico, comes a sturdy flat-bottom boat the Cajuns call a "pirogue," pronounced "pea-roh." In culinary circles, it's a canoe-shaped vegetable (usually eggplant and sometimes zucchini) stuffed with something delicious.

GINGER GRILLED PORK TENDERLOIN
with Peppered Walnuts and Bananas with Charred Pineapple Fried Rice | Serves 4

I have never felt that the description of this dish would help sell it, so it's never been on our regular printed menu. But whenever we run it as a special, we give our servers a taste so they can describe it to guests. Their enthusiasm about the flavor combination causes it to sell out almost every time!

Ingredients:
2 pounds pork tenderloin
½ cup dry Sherry wine
¼ cup tamari soy sauce
¼ cup balsamic vinegar
1 tablespoon Sambal Oelek
½ cup brown sugar
2 tablespoons fresh ginger root, peeled and minced
1 teaspoon garlic, minced
2 tablespoons safflower oil
1½ cups Serrano Pico de Gallo (see recipe)
3 bananas, peeled and sliced
1 cup Peppered Walnuts (see recipe)
Fresh cilantro leaves

CHEF'S NOTE: *Spend a little more on "good" soy sauce, Japanese tamari, and you'll be investing in richer, less salty and more complex flavors.*

Preparation:
1. Trim away any silverskin from the pork. Cut tenderloins lengthwise into strips about ½-inch thick and about 8 inches long. Tap lightly with a meat mallet to flatten strips just a bit.

2. Place pork strips in a shallow non-reactive (glass or stainless) baking dish. Cover and refrigerate until ready to grill.

3. Whisk together Sherry, soy sauce, vinegar, Sambal, brown sugar, ginger, garlic and oil in a small bowl. Equally divide the marinade into 2 separate containers.

4. Bring grill to medium-high heat and lightly oil the cooking grate so the pork doesn't stick.

5. Add half of the marinade to the pork strips, submerging the pork for 3 minutes — no longer. Drain and discard the used marinade.

6. Grill pork for 2–3 minutes per side to medium. Remove from grill and keep warm.

7. Heat a medium-sized sauté pan over medium-high heat and add oil. Toss in Serrano Pico de Gallo and sauté briefly. Add bananas, Peppered Walnuts and the other half of the marinade. Heat and stir gently until banana slices are warm and well glazed.

8. Arrange pork on serving platter and top with banana sauce. Garnish with fresh cilantro.

Serrano Pico De Gallo
Yield: About 1 cup

We like food that bites back, so I leave the seeds in the serrano. If you want a slightly milder taste, simply remove the seeds and membrane from the pepper before mincing.

Ingredients:
½ cup yellow onions, ¼-inch dice
½ cup Roma tomatoes, ¼-inch dice
2 serrano chiles, minced
¼ bunch fresh cilantro, minced
1 tablespoon olive oil
Kosher salt and freshly ground black pepper

Preparation:
Mix all ingredients in a small bowl and season with salt and pepper.

Peppered Walnuts
Yield: 1 cup

Ingredients:
1 cup walnut halves
1 teaspoon unsalted butter, melted
2 teaspoons granulated sugar
¼ teaspoon chili powder
1 teaspoon course ground black pepper
Kosher salt

Preparation:
1. Preheat oven to 350°.

2. Mix all ingredients in a small bowl, coating walnuts well.

3. Spread nuts in a single layer on a baking sheet and bake for about 5 minutes or until nuts are lightly toasted.

4. Allow walnuts to cool. Store in an airtight container until ready to use.

Charred Pineapple Fried Rice
Serves 4–6 (or 2 of my kids)

We like to use a blend of white and wild rice, but any non-sticky rice will work fine. Grilling the pineapple adds an extra dimension of taste to the dish, but if you're making this when your grill isn't hot, char the pineapple ring in a hot cast-iron skillet instead. You won't get the smoky flavor the grill imparts, but you will get the caramelized char.

Ingredients:
1 fresh pineapple slice, about ½-inch thick
1 teaspoon Cabernet Grill Dry Rub
1 tablespoon safflower oil
2 cloves garlic, minced
2 teaspoons fresh ginger root, minced
¼ cup Tasso ham, ⅛-inch dice
¼ cup red bell pepper, ⅛-inch dice
2 cups day-old white Texmati rice or white/wild rice blend
1 egg
3 green onions, trimmed, sliced on the bias into ¼-inch slices
1 teaspoon toasted sesame oil
2 tablespoons tamari soy sauce

Preparation:
1. Prepare a charbroil grill with oak or hickory and bring the fire to medium-high heat.

2. Season the pineapple with the Cabernet Grill Dry Rub. Place pineapple directly over the flames, cooking until lightly charred. Turn slice over to char the other side, then remove and cool.

3. Remove the pineapple core (if present) and cut the pineapple into ½-inch dice to make about ½ cup of charred, diced pineapple.

4. Add safflower oil to a large skillet or wok on medium-high heat. Add the garlic and ginger; sauté briefly for about 30 seconds.

5. Add the Tasso ham and red bell pepper; sauté for an additional minute. Add the rice and pineapple and sauté for a couple more minutes, until the rice is hot.

6. Push the rice to one side of the pan and crack the egg into the empty part of the pan. Scramble the egg quickly, but do not overcook it to a dry consistency.

7. Pull the rice mixture back into the scrambled egg. Add the green onions, tamari and sesame oil. Toss together well and remove from heat. Serve immediately.

TEXAS RICE

Texans have been farming rice since about 1685, primarily in counties southeast of Fredericksburg along the upper Texas coast. The state's paddies produce about 7% of the nation's supply of rice — most of it the long-grain variety. I prefer to support Texas farmers and ranchers, so I always look for "Grown in the USA Rice" from Texas.

TEXAS LAMB DUO: ROSEMARY GRILLED AND MALBEC-BRAISED DORPER LAMB

with Maytag Blue/White Bean Ragout | Serves 4

Lamb is versatile and flavorful — no wonder it's popular in cultures around the world. This dish showcases the differences in texture and flavors you can coax from the meat, and how well it matches with strong flavors like rosemary, Bleu cheese and hearty red wine.

Rosemary Grilled Lamb Chops

Ingredients:
1 Dorper lamb rack
1 tablespoon fresh rosemary, minced
4 cloves garlic, minced
2 tablespoons balsamic vinegar
½ cup olive oil (not extra virgin)
Kosher salt and freshly ground black pepper

Preparation:
1. Trim silverskin from rack and cut rack into individual chops. Place in a non-reactive (glass or stainless steel) pan.

2. Mix rosemary, garlic, vinegar and oil. Pour over lamb and allow to marinate for at least 2 hours or overnight, refrigerated.

3. Drain marinade and season lamb with salt and pepper.

4. Place chops on a hot charbroil grill and cook to medium-rare.

Malbec-Braised Lamb Shoulder

Ingredients:
2 tablespoons safflower oil
2 teaspoons kosher salt
2 pounds Dorper lamb shoulder, boneless
⅓ cup celery, ½-inch dice
⅓ cup carrots, peeled, ½-inch dice
⅔ cup onions, peeled, ½-inch dice
2 cloves garlic, smashed
1 teaspoon freshly ground black pepper
2 teaspoons ground cumin
2 teaspoons ground pasilla chile powder
½ teaspoon fresh oregano
½ teaspoon crushed red pepper
1 bay leaf
½ cup chopped tomatoes
2 cups (divided use) Becker Vineyards Malbec
1 cup Veal Stock (See recipe page 76. Beef or chicken will work just as well)

Preparation:
1. Preheat oven to 325°.

2. Cut lamb shoulder into 3-inch chunks and season lightly with kosher salt.

3. Heat a heavy skillet over medium-high heat and add oil. Place a few pieces of lamb at a time in the skillet, browning on all sides. Remove meat from the skillet when it is browned, and place it a roasting pan. Repeat process until all the lamb is browned.

4. Add celery, carrots and onions to the same skillet and brown lightly. Add the garlic and spices; sauté briefly with the other vegetables.

5. Move vegetable mixture to the roasting pan with the lamb. Deglaze the skillet with 1 cup of wine, scraping the bottom of the pan to loosen all the browned bits of meat and vegetables. Drink the other cup of wine.

6. Pour deglazing liquid over the lamb and vegetables in the roasting pan. Add tomatoes and stock.

7. Cover pan tightly and place in a 325° oven to braise for 3–4 hours, or until lamb is completely tender and shreds easily with 2 forks. Allow lamb to cool in the braising liquid.

8. When the lamb has cooled, drain the braising liquid into a small saucepan, leaving the meat in the roasting pan. Reduce the liquid over a medium-high heat until it has a very light sauce-like consistency.

9. Shred all the lamb lightly with 2 forks, removing any large pieces of fat or gristle.

10. Place the meat back into the reduced braising liquid to reheat. Serve immediately.

Maytag Blue/White Bean Ragout

Ingredients:
1 tablespoon unsalted butter
¼ cup yellow onions, peeled, ¼-inch dice
2 cloves garlic, minced
¼ cup chicken stock
1 tablespoon fresh basil, minced
2 cups cooked Great Northern white beans
⅓ cup Maytag Blue cheese, crumbled
Kosher salt and freshly ground black pepper

Preparation:
1. Heat a small skillet over medium heat. Place butter in the pan to melt until it begins bubbling.

2. Add onions and garlic and sweat the vegetables until translucent. Do not brown them.

3. Add chicken stock and beans and heat through. Stir in basil and cheese. Adjust seasoning with salt and pepper.

TEXAS-BRED DORPER LAMB

I bought my first Texas Dorper lamb chops from Twin County Dorpers at the Fredericksburg Farmers Market, and quickly became enamored and curious about this local meat. You don't associate wool with the Texas heat, so I was surprised to find such tasty lamb in the temperate Hill Country. Turns out Dorper was bred in South Africa specifically to handle arid conditions. They don't need to be shorn like other wool-producing breeds, and the meat is never gamey like other breeds can be.

MAPLE-CURED SMOKED PORK TENDERLOIN
with Granny Smith Apple/Cranberry/Candied Pecan/Date Pan Sauce | Serves 4

You won't believe the layers of flavors in this dish. The brine starts it off, the low smoking process really gets it going and the Pan Sauce finishes it off in style. What also makes this dish special is the texture of the sauce, a mixture of tender fruits and firm Candied Pecans, in a maple-enriched velvety liquor. It is truly a crowd pleaser that I'm sure you'll enjoy making and serving time and again.

Ingredients:

2 pounds pork tenderloin, whole
2 quarts Maple Brown Sugar Brine (see recipe)
1 tablespoon unsalted butter
1 clove garlic, minced
½ shallot, minced
2 small Granny Smith apples, diced
2 tablespoons dried cranberries
12 pitted dates, sliced
1 ounce bourbon
1 cup Demi-glace
3 tablespoons unsalted butter, cold, divided use
2 tablespoons pure maple syrup
2 tablespoons Candied Pecans (see recipe)
Kosher salt and freshly ground black pepper

Preparation:

1. Trim away any silverskin and excess fat from the pork, or have your butcher do it for you. Place pork in brine and refrigerate for no more than 2 hours.

2. Set up smoker with oak wood, according to manufacturer's directions.

3. Remove pork from brine and pat dry with paper towels. Place meat in smoker and cook over medium-low heat for 30–40 minutes, or until the pork reaches medium on a meat thermometer.

4. Place 1 tablespoon of butter, garlic and shallots in a small sauté pan over medium heat; sauté briefly.

5. Add apples, cranberries and dates and cook for about 2 minutes, or until apples begin to soften slightly on the edges.

6. Add bourbon and ignite the liquid. Allow the alcohol to burn off, then add demi-glace to the pan. When the demi-glace comes to a full simmer, remove the pan from the heat and whip in the remaining 2 tablespoons of cold butter and the maple syrup.

7. Add the pecans to the sauce.

8. Season Pan Sauce with salt and pepper.

9. Slice pork tenderloins and arrange on a platter, topped with Pan Sauce.

It's Good to be Rare

Pork tastes better, is juicer and more flavorful, when prepared medium-rare. The days of well-done pork are long over—and have been since most danger was eradicated in the 1950s. If your pork always turns out dry, try cooking it to medium-rare and rediscover the flavor of this affordable and plentiful meat.

Maple Brown Sugar Brine
Yield: About 2 quarts

Ingredients:
1 quart water
½ cup kosher salt
¼ cup brown sugar
2 bay leaves
1 teaspoon black peppercorns, whole
2 cloves garlic, mashed
1 quart ice water
¼ cup pure maple syrup

Preparation:
1. Place all ingredients, except ice water and maple syrup, in a saucepan. Bring to a boil.

2. Remove from heat and add ice water and maple syrup.

3. Use to brine pork tenderloins for 2 hours—and no longer!

I like to brine pork before smoking it because it results in juicer meat with a deeper smoke flavor. The brine recipe is important in imparting some taste, but the key to better brining is timing. If you leave the pork in the brine any longer than 2 hours for this size and cut of meat, it will become salty and mealy. Remember this no matter what brining solution you use.

Candied Pecans
Yield: 4 cups

You'll only need a few nuts for the finished Pan Sauce. Good thing. You're probably going to snack on them as you cook. I know I do.

Ingredients:
1 egg white
4 cups pecan halves
2 tablespoons granulated sugar
¼ teaspoon kosher salt
¼ teaspoon freshly ground black pepper

Preparation:
1. Preheat oven to 350°.

2. Place the egg white in a medium-sized copper or stainless steel bowl; whip vigorously with a wire whisk for about 1 minute, or until soft peaks form.

3. Add the rest of the ingredients and toss until the pecans are well coated.

4. Pour the pecans onto 2 parchment-lined baking sheets in a single layer, being sure they are not crowded. Bake 12–15 minutes, or until nuts are crisp and lightly golden.

5. Allow to cool fully before serving.

DRY RUBBED CERTIFIED ANGUS BEEF TENDERLOIN TAILS

with Roasted Garlic Serrano Béarnaise and Potato Parsnip Gratin | Serves 6

Tenderloin tails have a funny shape, because they're cut off the ends of the larger tenderloin roast. They are as tender and tasty as tenderloin, and generally priced lower per pound. But they're gaining popularity, so you may have to argue the price with your butcher.

Ingredients:
3 pounds Certified Angus Beef tenderloin tails
½ cup Cabernet Grill Dry Rub
1¼ cups Roasted Garlic Serrano Béarnaise (see recipe)

Preparation:

1. Rub Cabernet Grill Dry Rub on all surfaces of tenderloin tails. Allow meat to rest in the refrigerator for at least 1 hour so flavors can penetrate.

2. While the meat is attaining maximum flavor, set some oak wood in a charbroil grill and allow it to burn until completely ashed over.

3. Cook tenderloin tails over hot oak fire to medium-rare and serve hot.

DISH ASSEMBLY: *Pour Béarnaise into a warm sauceboat and serve alongside tenderloin tails and Potato Parsnip Gratin. Béarnaise cannot be reheated and should be made just prior to serving.*

What Makes Certified Angus Beef So Superior

While we occasionally serve premium Akaushi or grass-fed beef as an extra treat, our everyday "go-to" beef has always been *Certified Angus Beef*© because I want to serve our guests a consistently top-quality product. Angus cattle develops with better, more evenly distributed marbling than most other breeds, which places *Certified Angus Beef*© in the top 10% of beef as determined by USDA quality standards. Beef is graded based on marbling, with the highest degree of marbling in the Prime grade (less than 3% of all beef). *Certified Angus Beef*© is strictly quality controlled and must be in the top 2 USDA grades: Prime (less than 3% of all beef) and Choice. It must also pass 8 additional quality checks in order to be labeled "Certified Angus Beef." It is this strict quality control and strong focus on consistently great flavor and texture that makes *Certified Angus Beef*© superior. I believe it is some of the best beef available.

SINCE 1978
CERTIFIED Angus BEEF®
BRAND

Roasted Garlic Serrano Béarnaise
Yield: Enough for 6 steaks

Ingredients:
2 serrano chiles, whole
1 head garlic, whole
1 tablespoon shallots, roughly chopped
¼ cup tarragon vinegar
1 tablespoon fresh Marigold Mint or Texas Tarragon
8 ounces unsalted butter
2 egg yolks
Kosher salt and freshly ground black pepper

Preparation:

1. Preheat oven to 350°.

2. Brush a piece of foil with oil. Place the garlic and serrano chiles on the foil and seal the packet. Place in oven and roast until they become soft, about 45 minutes.

3. Extract the roasted garlic by cutting off the top of the garlic head and squeezing the garlic pulp from its papery skin. Mash the pulp with the softened serrano chiles and set the mixture aside.

4. Place shallots, tarragon vinegar and herbs in a small saucepan over high heat. Reduce the liquid by two-thirds. Strain out and discard shallots and herbs, reserving only the reduced vinegar.

5. Meanwhile, melt the butter in another small saucepan and bring it to a rolling simmer over medium-high heat.

6. Place egg yolks in the bowl of a small food processor. With the motor running, pour in simmering butter—drop by drop—increasing to a thin steady stream until mixture is fully incorporated as a smooth emulsion, as thick as light mayonnaise.

   CHEF'S NOTE: *If the sauce "breaks" or separates into an oily mess, start over and add the butter in a slower stream.*

7. Leave the motor running as you add in the reserved vinegar reduction.

8. Add roasted garlic-serrano paste to taste (about a tablespoon should do) and season with salt and pepper.

TEXAS TARRAGON VS. FRENCH OR RUSSIAN TARRAGON

The Texas Tarragon (or Marigold Mint) we grow on the Cotton Gin Village grounds and use in the Cabernet Grill, is a native plant that blooms with small yellow flowers in late summer. Unlike French or Russian Tarragon, it thrives in our hot, dry climate; like the other varieties, it imparts a licorice or anise taste and aroma to foods.

Parsnip Potato Gratin
Serves 4

I don't know why more people don't eat parsnips. I am often asked what they taste like and, to me, they taste like a cross between a sweet carrot and a potato. I simply love parsnips — mashed, fried, boiled, roasted and or in a gratin. When you mix parsnips with potatoes, they add a whole new dimension to a gratin. I served this particular dish as an accompaniment to herb-crusted strip loin at a Texas Hills Vineyard vintner dinner and guest comments were over the top. I suspect you'll get the same response at your table.

Ingredients:
1 large russet potato (about 10 ounces), peeled, ⅛-inch slices
2 large parsnips (about 8 ounces), peeled, ⅛-inch slices
2 cups chicken stock or water
1 tablespoon unsalted butter
1 shallot, minced
¾ cup heavy cream
1 bay leaf
½ teaspoon fresh thyme
1 teaspoon kosher salt
¼ teaspoon freshly ground black pepper
½ cup Gruyere cheese, grated
½ cup Panko breadcrumbs
1 tablespoon unsalted butter, melted

Preparation:
1. Preheat oven to 350°. Heat chicken stock to boiling in a medium-sized saucepan. Add the sliced potatoes and cook for about 5 minutes or until fork-tender, but not overcooked and falling apart.

2. Use a slotted spoon to remove the potatoes from the stock and to a large bowl.

3. Bring liquid back to a boil and add the parsnips. The parsnips will probably cook a bit faster than the potatoes.

4. Remove from heat and drain the liquid from the parsnips. Toss parsnips and potatoes together and set aside.

5. In a small saucepan over medium heat, sweat the shallots in 1 tablespoon of butter for a few minutes until translucent, but not browned. Add heavy cream, herbs, salt and pepper and allow to simmer for 4 minutes to meld the flavors. Remove and discard bay leaf.

6. Butter the sides of a 6-inch round casserole dish. Alternate layers of parsnips and potatoes, cheese and cream.

7. Mix breadcrumbs with melted butter. Spread mixture evenly over the top of the casserole. Place casserole on a sheet pan in the center of the oven.

8. Cook at 350° for 30–40 minutes or until the breadcrumbs are golden brown, the casserole is bubbling on the sides, and a knife inserted in the center of the dish comes out hot.

9. Remove from oven and allow casserole to rest for 10 minutes before serving.

LOBSTER-TOPPED CHICKEN FRIED RIBEYE

with Shallot Cream Sauce and Cheddar-Scallion Smashed Potatoes | Serves 4

When I first opened the Cabernet Grill, I swore I wouldn't put a chicken fried steak on the menu because it was just too common of a dish, and my goal was to be unique. After thousands of requests, I broke down and added a chicken fried pork steak, hoping to satisfy guests while remaining true to my vision of being different. Despite the success of that dish, we still got request after request for chicken fried beef steak and cream gravy. After 10 years, I relented, but on my terms, with one of the most decadent CFS you'll ever encounter, using Certified Angus ribeye steak topped with lobster "cream gravy." It is the ultimate treat of two favorites on one plate, and one of the Cabernet Grill's best sellers.

Ingredients:

4 4-ounce lobster tails
3 tablespoons butter
1 shallot, minced
¼ cup water
¼ cup Texas Viognier wine
1 bay leaf
1 pinch fresh thyme
1 pinch freshly ground black pepper
4 8-ounce Certified Angus ribeye steaks
1 cup Seasoned Flour Mix (see recipe)
1 cup Seasoned Cracker Mix (see recipe)
2 eggs, beaten
½ cup roasted green chiles, seeded, peeled and diced
2 strips bacon, diced and cooked until almost crisp
1½ cups Shallot Cream Sauce (see recipe)
Peanut or safflower oil

Seasoned Flour Mix
Yield: ½ cup

Ingredients:
½ cup all-purpose flour
½ teaspoon black pepper
½ teaspoon granulated garlic
¼ teaspoon fresh thyme
½ tablespoon kosher salt

Preparation:
Mix all ingredients well.

Seasoned Cracker Mix
Yield: 1 cup

Ingredients:
½ cup all-purpose flour
½ cup cracker meal
1 teaspoon black pepper
1 teaspoon granulated garlic
½ teaspoon fresh thyme
2 teaspoons kosher salt

Preparation:
Mix all ingredients well.

Preparation:

1. Pull lobster meat from tails. (See *Treat Your Lobster Kindly*—next page—for instructions.)

2. Place butter and shallots into a small saucepan over medium-low heat. Cook slowly until shallots are translucent. Do not allow them to brown.

3. Add the water, wine, bay leaf, thyme, pepper and lobster tails and gently bring the temperature of the liquid up to 128° as slowly as possible, checking with an instant-read thermometer. Try to make this process last at least 15 minutes.

4. As soon as the liquid reaches 128°, begin to monitor the temperature of the lobster tails by placing the thermometer into the thickest part of one of the tails. Continue to cook the tails until the thermometer reaches 128°. (If you warmed the liquid slowly enough, the tails may already be at that temperature.)

5. Once at 128°, immediately drain them from the liquid and set the tails on a plate in the refrigerator, uncovered, to cool for about 20 minutes.

6. Dredge ribeye steaks on both sides in Seasoned Flour Mix. Shake off any excess flour.

7. Place individual steaks in an unsealed 1-gallon Ziploc bag and pound with a flat meat mallet until each is uniformly about ½-inch thick.

8. Put beaten eggs in a shallow dish and dip each ribeye steak in egg, coating both sides. Allow excess liquid to drain off.

9. Next, dredge each steak in Seasoned Cracker Mix and shake off any excess coating.

10. Pour peanut oil into a heavy skillet to a depth of 1 inch; heat over medium-high heat to 350°, or until a few breadcrumbs dropped in the oil sizzle and brown.

11. Cook 1 or 2 ribeyes at a time, without crowding in the oil, for about 3 minutes on each side, or until golden brown.

Cheddar-Scallion Smashed Potatoes

Serves about 6

Ingredients:

2 pounds russet potatoes
½ stick unsalted butter
⅔ cup heavy cream
⅓ cup extra sharp white cheddar cheese, grated
⅓ cup scallions, minced
Kosher salt and freshly ground black pepper

Preparation:

1. Preheat oven to 400°.

2. Wash potatoes well (but do not remove the skin) and cut into quarters. Place in a saucepan and cover with cold water.

3. Bring water to a boil, then reduce the heat to a simmer and cook potatoes until they are tender.

4. Pour potatoes into a colander and drain off the water. While the potatoes are still hot, turn them onto a sheet pan and place them in the preheated oven for about 4 minutes. This will dry the potatoes completely.

5. Place potatoes in a large mixing bowl and mash them with butter, cream, cheese and scallions.

6. Adjust the seasoning with salt and pepper.

Shallot Cream Sauce

Yield: 1½ cups

Ingredients:

½ cup shallots, minced
2 tablespoons safflower oil
½ cup Texas Viognier white wine
2 cups heavy cream
½ teaspoon Tabasco Sauce
Kosher salt and freshly ground black pepper

Preparation:

1. Place a small, heavy-bottomed saucepan on medium-low heat. Add shallots and oil.

2. Sweat the shallots until translucent, stirring often. Do not allow shallots to brown.

3. Add wine and increase heat to medium-high.

4. Allow wine and shallot mixture to reduce by about 80%.

5. Add cream and continue to cook, reducing mixture by 25%.

6. Remove from heat and strain out shallots.

7. Place sauce back over low heat and add Tabasco Sauce. Whisk mixture to combine well; adjust seasoning with salt and pepper.

DISH ASSEMBLY: *While the steaks are cooking, heat Shallot Cream Sauce in a small saucepan, and add roasted chiles and bacon. Cut lobster tails into ⅓-inch slices; add to sauce and simmer for a couple of minutes until just heated through. Do not allow the sauce to boil or the lobster will become tough. To serve: Top each chicken fried steak with lobster gravy. Serve alongside a large dollop of Cheddar-Scallion Smashed Potatoes.*

Treat Your Lobster Kindly

For this dish, you'll remove the lobster meat from its shell before you cook it. If you cook it in the shell, the meat will stick to the shell and you'll have a hard time getting solid, uniform chunks of meat. Just use kitchen shears to cut a slit down the center of the softest side of the raw tail. Pull each side of the shell away and the meat should come right out. Whether you cook lobster in or out of its shell, avoid turning the meat into a rubbery mess by treating it with kindness. Pamper it with a slow build to an extra-hot bath—don't shock it by plunging it into harsh, boiling water.

COCONUT CRUSTED SHRIMP
with Five-Pepper Glaze and Jalapeño Red Onion Slaw | Serves 4

The Cabernet Grill has been dedicated to serving only Texas wild-caught shrimp since the day we opened our doors. My friend Bobby Champion, the State Coordinator for Texas Shrimp Marketing, has a good explanation of why Texas wild-caught shrimp are so delicious.

"We close the Texas Gulf fishing waters for two months, from May 15 through July 15, so the shrimp can repopulate and grow. That's one thing. But it's also the passion of the shrimpers who are out on their boats for 30–60 days at a time. They respect the waters and the shrimp, and are a large part of keeping the ecosystem balanced the water healthy."

Bobby told me about a blind taste test they did of farm raised, imported and Texas wild-caught shrimp. The Texas wild-caught won hands-down for their sweet, robust and briny flavor. I think they're everything you want in shrimp and make a big difference in a dish. That's why Texas wild-caught are the only shrimp you'll find at the Cabernet Grill.

Ingredients:

2 pounds jumbo Texas wild-caught shrimp
1½ cups Panko breadcrumbs
1½ cups unsweetened coconut, shredded
1 cup all-purpose flour
2 teaspoons Cabernet Grill Cajun Seasoning
2 eggs, lightly beaten
1 cup milk
2 teaspoons Cabernet Grill Cajun Seasoning
1 cup Five-Pepper Glaze (see recipe)
Peanut oil

Preparation:

1. Peel the shrimp, leaving the tail shells intact.

2. Butterfly the shrimp by running a paring knife down the back of each one. Remove the dark vein.

3. Pat the shrimp dry with paper towels and keep them refrigerated until you are ready to bread them.

4. Set up a breading station: Mix the breadcrumbs and coconut in a small bowl. In a separate bowl, mix flour and 2 teaspoons of Cabernet Grill Cajun Seasoning. In a third bowl, mix eggs, milk and 2 teaspoons of Cabernet Grill Cajun Seasoning.

5. Place shrimp in flour mixture and toss to coat. Shake off any excess flour. You will need to coat the shrimp in batches to ensure they get coated evenly.

6. Dip shrimp individually into egg mixture; allow excess to drip off, then place shrimp in coconut breading mixture.

7. Press the coconut breading onto the shrimp, coating all sides well. Continue the process until all the shrimp are breaded.

8. Add enough peanut oil to a deep fryer or heavy pot so shrimp can be submerged in at least 3 inches of oil. Heat the oil to 350°.

9. When the oil reaches the proper temperature, add the coated shrimp in small batches, cooking about 1 minute or so, until golden brown.

10. Scoop the shrimp from the fryer and drain on paper towel or a wire rack, then keep warm on a warmed platter. Continue until all the shrimp are cooked.

11. Toss shrimp in heated Five-Pepper Glaze. Drain any excess glaze and serve immediately.

Five-Pepper Glaze
Yield: About 1 cup

Ingredients:

¾ cup light corn syrup
¾ cup white wine vinegar
1 tablespoon safflower oil
1 tablespoon fresh jalapeños, minced
¼ cup red bell pepper, ¼-inch dice
¼ cup poblano chile, ¼-inch dice
½ teaspoon medium-grind black pepper
½ teaspoon crushed red pepper
1 tablespoon shallots, minced
1 teaspoon garlic, minced

Preparation:

1. Place corn syrup and vinegar in a small saucepan over medium-high heat; reduce volume by 50% or until the syrup coats a cold spoon inserted quickly into it.

2. Remove from heat and keep sauce warm.

3. Meanwhile, heat a small skillet over medium heat, add the oil, and sauté all the remaining ingredients for 3–4 minutes until softened just a bit. Stir sauté into the syrup to distribute the peppers well.

4. Refrigerate for future use or heat back up a bit and use immediately.

Jalapeño Red Onion Slaw

Serves 4–6

Ingredients:

2 cups red cabbage, shredded
½ cup carrots, shredded
1 tablespoon fresh jalapeños, minced
1 tablespoon fresh cilantro, minced
2 cups red onions, sliced very thin
⅓ cup red wine vinegar
⅓ cup granulated sugar
2 tablespoons safflower oil
1 clove garlic, minced
Kosher salt and freshly ground black pepper

Preparation:

1. Mix all ingredients in a medium-sized bowl until well incorporated.

2. Season with salt and pepper.

3. Refrigerate at least 15 minutes before serving.

THE CORRECT COCONUT

Look for the finest shred of unsweetened coconut you can find. We use a "baker's thread shred" for this recipe, but flake will do just fine. The most important thing is to be sure you get unsweetened coconut. Sweetened coconut is combined with confectioner's sugar, and that will make the coating turn brown in the oil, plus make the dish way too sweet. If you can't find unsweetened coconut at your grocery store, it is available online.

TEXAS WILD-CAUGHT SHRIMP
with Curried Pineapple Crema and Cilantro Pomegranate Couscous | Serves 6–8

The Spaniards brought pomegranates to cultivate in Texas in the 16th century, and now they also grow wild here, blooming with red, sweet fruit in the fall. We have a few of these beautiful shrubs planted on the Cotton Gin Village grounds, and I'd like to say I harvest the fruit and use those seeds when I make this dish. The fact is, though, the birds and squirrels always get to the ripe fruit before I do!

Ingredients:

1 tablespoon safflower oil
2 tablespoons shallots, minced
1 tablespoon fresh ginger root, minced
1 tablespoon curry powder
¼ cup freshly-squeezed lime juice
1 lime, zested
¼ cup white wine
2 cups pineapple, crushed
1 teaspoon crushed red pepper
½ cup habanero or spicy jalapeño jelly
2 cups heavy cream or Mexican crema
Kosher salt
Fresh cilantro, minced (optional)
3 pounds jumbo Texas wild-caught shrimp,
    peeled and deveined
2 tablespoons safflower oil
2 cloves garlic, minced
Kosher salt and freshly ground black pepper

Preparation:
For the Curried Pineapple Crema:

1. Heat 1 tablespoon of oil in heavy-bottomed saucepan over medium heat.

2. Add shallots and ginger; sauté briefly, not allowing them to brown.

3. Add curry powder and stir, continuing to sauté for 1 minute until the curry becomes fragrant.

4. Deglaze the saucepan with lime juice, zest and white wine. Allow mixture to reduce in volume by two-thirds.

5. Mix in pineapple, red pepper, habanero jelly and crema. Bring mixture to a low boil and reduce volume by one-third.

6. Adjust seasoning and stir in cilantro if desired.

For the Shrimp:

1. Heat 2 tablespoons of oil in sauté pan over medium-high heat. Add garlic and sauté briefly.

2. Add shrimp to pan in batches; season with salt and pepper.

3. Cook shrimp for about 3 minutes, until it has curled slightly, turned pink and the center is no longer translucent.

Cilantro Pomegranate Couscous

Yield: About 2 cups

Ingredients:

1 tablespoon unsalted butter
2 cloves garlic, minced
1 cup chicken stock
1 cup couscous, uncooked
¼ cup fresh pomegranate seeds
2 tablespoons fresh cilantro, minced
Kosher salt and freshly ground black pepper

Preparation:

1. Melt butter in a small saucepan over medium heat. Add the garlic; cook slowly to soften the garlic but do not allow it to brown.

2. When the garlic is soft, add the chicken stock and bring the mixture to a boil. Stir in the couscous, remove from the heat and cover. Allow to rest for 5 minutes.

3. Stir in pomegranate seeds and cilantro; adjust seasoning with salt and pepper. Serve hot.

DISH ASSEMBLY: *Set out individual shallow serving bowls. Place a scoop of Cilantro Pomegranate Couscous in the center of each bowl. Arrange shrimp in a circle around the couscous, ladle Curried Pineapple Crema over couscous and shrimp, and garnish with additional pomegranate seeds and cilantro.*

RUSTLIN' ROB'S GOURMET FOODS

I developed this dish because I had a lot of habanero jelly. Why? Rob Simpson of Rustlin' Rob's Gourmet Foods on Main Street gave me 6 cases of the sweet/hot stuff to play with. And since I know Rob loves shrimp, I came up with this dish in his honor. If you love to cook and love to eat, you'll get lost in the aisles at Rustlin' Rob's. It's a lot of fun, and Rob is someone you just have to meet. He's a true Fredericksburg treasure.

PAN SEARED PORK CUTLETS
with Roasted Garlic, Mushrooms, Porcini Cream Sauce and Gorgonzola | Serves 4

What I love about this dish is how well the earthy Italian elements—garlic, porcini mushrooms, rosemary and gorgonzola—match with smooth Texas Sangiovese wine. Most Italian varietals grow exceptionally well in the Texas Hill Country because the grapes thrive in a hot and sunny growing environment, and because Tuscan and Hill Country soils and terrains are very similar. I especially like pairing this dish with a few glasses of Sangiovese from Texas Hills Vineyard—where owners/winemakers Gary and Kathy Gilstrap's passion for Mediterranean-style grapes has put their winery, and Super Texan wines, on the map.

Ingredients:
1½ pounds center-cut pork loin
¾ cup all-purpose flour
2 teaspoons Cabernet Grill Cajun Seasoning
3 tablespoons safflower oil
3 tablespoons unsalted butter
2 cups crimini mushrooms, sliced
2 tablespoons Texas Sangiovese wine
1 cup Porcini Cream Sauce (see recipe)
⅓ cup Roasted Garlic cloves (see recipe)
2 tablespoons fresh chives, minced
Kosher salt and freshly ground black pepper
½ cup gorgonzola cheese, crumbled

Preparation:
1. Slice the pork loin into ½-inch thick medallions, then stack them up neatly. Slice the stack in half so that you have twice as many half-moon pieces.

2. Place a few pieces of pork at a time into an unsealed 1-gallon Ziploc bag, keeping pieces flat in one layer. Beat with a meat mallet until they are about ¼-inch thick. Repeat until all meat has been flattened.

3. Mix flour and Cabernet Grill Cajun Seasoning in a shallow bowl. Dredge each pork in seasoned flour and shake off any excess flour.

4. Heat a large skillet over medium-high heat and add half of the safflower oil and butter. As soon as the butter begins to sizzle and turns a bit brown on the edges, add a single layer of pork medallions to the pan. Cook for 1–2 minutes per side. The pork should be a medium pink on the inside.

5. Remove cooked pork cutlets from the pan and transfer to a warm platter. Repeat, using the remaining oil and butter as needed, until all the pork medallions are cooked and arranged on the platter.

6. Add the mushrooms to the pan and sauté for a couple of minutes until they begin to soften and turn golden on the edges. Leave the mushrooms in the pan as you deglaze the pan with wine, using a spatula to scrape up any browned bits on the bottom of the pan.

7. Turn the heat to medium and add in the Porcini Cream Sauce, roasted garlic and chives. Stir for a couple of minutes until the sauce is hot. Adjust seasoning with salt and pepper.

8. Pour the finished sauce over the pork medallions and top with gorgonzola cheese.

9. Serve immediately.

Roasted Garlic
Yield: About ¾ cup

Ingredients:
1 tablespoon virgin olive oil
1 cup whole garlic cloves, peeled
Kosher salt

Preparation:
1. Preheat oven to 350°.

2. Cut a 12-inch x 12-inch sheet of heavy duty aluminum foil and pour the olive oil in the center of the sheet. Use your fingers or a brush to spread the olive oil into a 6-inch circle in the center of the foil.

3. Place garlic cloves onto the oil circle and fold the edges up in both directions to form an envelope. Seal all the edges of the foil.

4. On a small baking pan or medium size skillet, pour salt to a layer at least ½-inch deep. This salt layer will keep the garlic from burning.

5. Place the foil packet on top of the salt and place the pan in the oven. Cook for 50–60 minutes.

6. When done, the garlic should be soft and creamy when pressed with a fork. If it is still firm, cook a bit longer.

7. Garlic can be frozen in a Ziploc bag if not being used immediately. Store the salt and use it when you roast garlic again.

Porcini Cream Sauce | Yield: About 1¼ cups

The earthy, nutty, creamy and aromatic qualities of Porcini mushrooms have made them an indispensable ingredient in gourmet kitchens. Cooking them with Sangiovese is a pairing made in heaven.

Ingredients:
1 shallot, minced
1 tablespoon safflower oil
⅓ cup or ¾-ounce dried porcini mushrooms
½ cup Texas Sangiovese wine
1 teaspoon fresh rosemary, minced
1 cup veal demi-glace
½ cup heavy cream
½ teaspoon freshly-squeezed lemon juice
Kosher salt and freshly ground black pepper

Preparation:
1. Add oil and shallots to a small saucepan over medium-low heat. Cook slowly, until the shallots become soft and translucent. Do not allow shallots to brown.

2. Add porcini mushrooms, wine and rosemary and increase the heat to medium-high. Reduce the liquid until the pan is almost dry. This process won't take much time because the mushrooms are going to soak up about half of the wine, so keep your eye on the saucepan.

3. Add demi-glace and continue to reduce the liquid by a third. Add the cream and continue to reduce the liquid until the sauce is thick enough to lightly coat the back of a spoon.

4. Use an immersion blender to puree the sauce in the pan until it is fairly smooth and creamy, or carefully puree the mixture in a blender or food processor.

5. Adjust the seasoning with lemon juice, salt and pepper. Serve hot.

Don't Buy Pre-Chopped Garlic

I hate peeling and chopping garlic as much as the next guy. Actually, I probably hate it more than the next guy. It's tedious, messy and way too time-consuming. But that's no excuse for using pre-chopped garlic in a jar. By the time it reaches the store — and with all the preservatives they use to keep it shelf-stable — it barely resembles true garlic. It can impart a bitter aftertaste to food — not an aromatic richness that real, fresh garlic adds. Do yourself a favor and take the time to buy and use garlic the way Mother Nature made it. Peeling it and chopping it is just part of the deal you make with her for letting you cook with it.

PECAN CRUSTED BREAST OF CHICKEN
with Creole Mustard Sauce and Savory Sweet Potato Spoonbread | Serves 4

Seriously, if I had a dime for every portion of this dish I served before I opened my own restaurant, I'd be living large! This classic chicken dish has served me well for banquets, weddings, private dining and as a restaurant menu item. The sauce adds life to mild chicken, and the pecans add another dimension to the breading. It really is pretty hard to beat as a crowd-pleaser.

Ingredients:
1½ cups fresh breadcrumbs (see Chef's Note)
½ cup pecan pieces, chopped semi-fine
1½ pounds small chicken breasts,
    boneless/skinless/trimmed
Kosher salt and freshly ground black pepper
1 tablespoon unsalted butter
1 tablespoon safflower oil
1 cup Creole Mustard Sauce (see recipe)
1 tablespoon fresh chives, minced

CHEF'S NOTE: *There is a big difference between the can of dry breadcrumbs hidden in the back of your cupboard and the breadcrumbs in this recipe. To make fresh breadcrumbs, just place a few slices of fresh bread in a food processor and pulse until the bread has a semi-fine consistency. You can use any cheap white bread; even hot dog buns work fine. Fresh, soft breadcrumbs give the chicken a lighter breading texture and allow the flavor of the pecans to come through.*

Preparation:
1. Mix breadcrumbs and pecans in a small bowl.

2. Season the chicken breasts lightly with salt and pepper.

3. Spread a layer of breadcrumb mix on a plate. Place a couple of chicken breasts on the breadcrumbs, then add more breading mix to the top of the chicken.

4. Use the heel of your hand to smash the breading into the chicken breasts, fully coating both sides.

5. Continue this process with the remaining chicken breasts. Throw away any breading mixture remaining on the plate when you're done.

6. Add butter and oil to a heavy sauté pan over medium heat.

7. Cook chicken breasts in a single layer until they turn golden brown; turn over to brown the other side. Cook until chicken has reached an internal temperature of 165°, or until the juices from the chicken run clear when the meat is pierced with a small knife. As pieces are done, move them to a warm serving platter.

8. Once all chicken breasts are cooked and on the platter, top with Creole Mustard Sauce and garnish with chives.

MOIST AND TENDER CHICKEN
If you find your chicken always turns out tough or dry or bland, take a look at the quality of the meat you're buying. Consider switching to pastured or free-range chicken, raised in lush fields, getting fresh air as they forage for seeds and insects to supplement their grain diet. Ask at your farmers market for local poultry and you'll see what a big difference freshness and animal care can make to the moistness, texture and flavor of your next chicken dish.

Creole Mustard Sauce | Yield: about 1 cup

Ingredients:

¼ cup shallots, minced
2 tablespoons safflower oil
½ cup Texas Viognier white wine
1 cup heavy cream
2 tablespoons Zatarain's Creole Mustard
1 teaspoon Tabasco Sauce
Kosher salt and freshly ground black pepper

Preparation:

1. Add shallots and oil to a small heavy-bottomed saucepan over medium-low heat.

2. Sweat shallots until translucent, stirring often. Do not allow shallots to brown.

3. Add white wine and increase heat to medium-high. Allow wine and shallot mixture to reduce by about 80%.

4. Add heavy cream and reduce mixture by 25%.

5. Remove pan from heat and pour sauce through a strainer to remove shallots.

6. Place sauce back in the saucepan over low heat; add mustard and Tabasco. Whisk mixture to incorporate.

7. Adjust seasoning with salt and pepper.

Savory Sweet Potato Spoonbread | Serves 6

A moist, delicious spoonbread doesn't always have to be made with cornmeal, though most people associate the two. I like the way this dish holds its own and complements the Pecan Crusted Chicken.

Ingredients:

1 tablespoon unsalted butter
2 cups sweet potatoes, cooked, cut into 1-inch chunks
2 cups day-old bread, cut into 1-inch chunks
2 tablespoons fresh chives, minced
1 cup aged white cheddar
3 strips bacon, cooked, crumbled
3 eggs, lightly beaten
½ cup brown sugar
1½ cups heavy cream
¼ teaspoon ground allspice
1 teaspoon kosher salt
½ teaspoon freshly ground black pepper
1 tablespoon unsalted butter, melted
2 tablespoons walnuts, chopped fine
¼ cup breadcrumbs

Preparation:

1. Preheat oven to 350°.

2. Brush the inside of an 8-inch casserole with butter.

3. Fold sweet potato, bread, chives, cheddar and bacon together in casserole dish.

4. In a small bowl, mix eggs, brown sugar, cream and spices; pour mixture over mixture in the casserole dish.

5. Bake 40–50 minutes or until a knife inserted into the center of the spoonbread comes out clean. Remove from oven and turn the heat up to 375°.

6. Mix butter, walnuts and breadcrumbs in a small bowl; spread on top of hot spoonbread and return it to the oven until lightly brown. Serve hot.

TEXAS PECANS

The official state tree of Texas: Pecan. Official nut of Texas: Pecan. These majestic trees predate humans in the region—and provide us with some of the shade we need as well as a bounty of nuts for our diet. Texas is the country's largest producer of native pecans—my favorite kind. I prefer San Saba pecans, a smaller nut in a hard shell, because the flavor is richer and the nut meatier. Folks in San Saba (about an hour north of Fredericksburg) claim to have a hundreds-of-years-old "mother pecan tree" from which modern varieties have been spliced.

RHUBARB-PORT GLAZED PORK COUNTRY RIBS

and Crispy Potato Latkes | Serves 6

When I was a little kid, the neighborhood half-pint gang and I would sneak stalks of rhubarb from our neighbor's garden across the street. We would put plenty of sugar in Dixie cups and dip the raw rhubarb stalk into the sugar, adding some sweetness to the tart fruit. We'd nibble on it and have puckered cheeks all day long! When fresh rhubarb isn't in season, you can use frozen chunks and the recipe will work just fine. But fresh is better—and don't forget to put some sugar in a Dixie cup and eat some raw while you cook.

Ingredients:

4 pounds boneless country pork ribs
Kosher salt and freshly ground black pepper
2 cups pork or chicken stock
1 cup yellow onions, diced
1 stalk celery, diced
3 cloves garlic, minced
1 bay leaf
⅓ cup brown sugar
⅓ cup Heinz Chili Sauce
1 cup Texas Port wine
1½ cups rhubarb, sliced
2 tablespoons chipotle puree
2 tablespoons safflower oil

Crispy Potato Latkes
Serves 6

Ingredients:

1½ pounds russet baking potatoes, peeled
¼ cup shallots, minced
¼ cup yellow onions, minced
1 whole egg
1 egg yolk
Kosher salt and freshly ground black pepper
Safflower oil

LATKE SUCCESS

There are several keys to making good, crispy potato pancakes. First, use a starchy potato—russet/baking potatoes work best—and not a waxy variety like white, Yukon Gold or red potatoes. Next, be sure your oil is hot (use vegetable oil, not olive oil) before you put the potatoes into the pan. Finally, wait until the first side is really golden brown and crispy before you flip the pancake. Never flip pancakes more than once.

Preparation:

1. Preheat oven to 350°.

2. Season ribs with salt and pepper; sauté in a hot pan until well-browned on all sides.

3. Place browned ribs in an ovenproof dish. Add stock, onions, celery, garlic and bay leaf. Cover pan tightly with a lid or foil and cook 1½–2 hours or longer, until the meat nearly falls apart when tested with a fork.

4. Make the Rhubarb-Port Glaze as the ribs cook. Place brown sugar, chili sauce, port wine, rhubarb, chipotle puree and oil in a saucepan and bring to a boil. Reduce heat to simmer and cook on a low simmer for 30 minutes.

5. When ribs are done, drain any remaining liquid from the pan and pour Rhubarb-Port Glaze over meat. Return ribs to the oven, uncovered, for 30 minutes, basting several times with the glaze. Serve hot.

Preparation:

1. Coarsely grate the potatoes. Place in a large bowl of cold water for a couple of minutes.

2. Drain water and place potatoes in a kitchen towel. Wring out as much moisture as possible from the potatoes.

3. Lightly beat together whole egg and egg yolk.

4. Place potatoes into a large bowl and mix with onions, shallots and beaten eggs. Season with salt and pepper.

5. Add ¼-inch of oil to a medium-sized skillet. Heat over medium-high heat.

6. Divide the potato mixture into 6 piles, placing half the piles in the hot oil. Press down with a spatula to make "potato pancakes."

7. Reduce heat to medium and cook about 4 minutes on each side, or until golden brown and crispy.

8. Drain latkes on paper towels and repeat the process with the next batch. Serve immediately.

TEXAS TARRAGON
SHRIMP SCAMPI
with Jalapeño Three-Cheese Grits | Serves 4

There's a lot of Lone Star flavor in this dish, from the wild-caught shrimp and native Texas Tarragon, to the crisp Texas Viognier wine, and down to the jalapeño-infused grits. If this dish doesn't take your taste buds on a journey to the Texas Hill Country, I don't know what will.

Ingredients:

2 pounds large Texas wild-caught shrimp, peeled and deveined

Kosher salt and freshly ground black pepper

8 cloves garlic, minced

2 tablespoons extra virgin olive oil

1 tablespoon Texas Tarragon (Marigold Mint) leaves, minced (see page 126)

20 grape tomatoes, cut in half (optional)

1 lemon, zested and juiced

½ cup Texas Viognier white wine

1 stick unsalted butter, chilled and sliced

Jalapeño Three Cheese Grits (see recipe)

2 scallions, green tops only, thinly sliced

Preparation:

1. Heat a large skillet over medium-high heat and add olive oil. Immediately add shrimp and top with garlic. Shake the pan to keep the shrimp from sticking.

2. Season the shrimp with salt and pepper, then add tarragon. Sauté until shrimp start to curl, turn pink and begin to turn opaque in the center.

3. Add the grape tomatoes (if using), plus lemon juice and zest. Stir. Add wine.

4. Once the liquid is simmering and the shrimp are about 90% cooked through, add butter, shaking the pan back and forth to form a creamy sauce.

Jalapeño Three-Cheese Grits
Serves 6

Some people argue that you must use long-cooking stone-ground grits if you want the utmost respect as a chef. I say phooey! Quick grits work great and this recipe will prove it. However, anyone who uses "instant grits" just might be deported from the Great State of Texas. Instant grits are truly awful. Keep your distance.

Ingredients:

2½ cups chicken stock

¾ cup quick grits (not instant)

⅓ cup Texas goat cheese, crumbled

⅓ cup white cheddar cheese, grated

⅓ cup Asiago cheese, grated

¼ cup heavy cream

1 tablespoon unsalted butter

1 fresh jalapeño, finely minced

Kosher salt and freshly ground pepper

Preparation:

1. Bring chicken stock to a full boil and whisk in grits.

2. Turn heat down to medium-low; allow grits to simmer for about 10 minutes, stirring frequently.

3. Remove grits from heat and stir in all cheeses, cream, butter and jalapeños. Season with salt and pepper.

DISH ASSEMBLY: *Place a heaping spoonful of Jalapeño Three Cheese Grits into warm bowls. Ladle shrimp and sauce over and top with scallions. Serve immediately.*

PAN SEARED RAINBOW TROUT

Stuffed with Roasted Tomatoes, Asiago Cheese, Fresh Herbs and Applewood Smoked Bacon, Toasted Pecan Butter Sauce and Rosemary Cajun Bliss Potatoes | Serves 4

Nothing beats the flavor of fresh fish straight from the stream. If your fishing expedition doesn't work out as planned, or you can't find whole rainbow trout at your market, use boneless sole fillets for this recipe. Just "stuff" two fillets like a sandwich and the results will be just as delicious.

Ingredients:

2 Roma tomatoes
2 cups fresh breadcrumbs
4 strips applewood smoked bacon,
   cooked crisp and crumbled
¼ cup Asiago cheese, grated
1 tablespoon unsalted butter, melted
1 tablespoon fresh basil, chiffonade cut
2 tablespoons fresh chives, minced
1 tablespoon fresh parsley, minced
½ teaspoon freshly ground black pepper
4 whole rainbow trout, boneless
1 cup yellow cornmeal
1 tablespoon Cabernet Grill Cajun Seasoning
4 tablespoons safflower oil
1 cup Toasted Pecan Butter (see recipe)

Preparation:

1. Preheat broiler to high.

2. Cut tomatoes in half lengthwise and coat with a little bit of cooking spray or salad oil and place on a small pan under the broiler, skin side up. Broil until the tomato skins start to darken or blister and the tomato flesh softens. Remove from broiler and allow to cool.

3. Remove skin and any excess seeds that have released from the tomatoes. Chop roughly and place in a medium-sized bowl. Add breadcrumbs, bacon, cheese, melted butter, herbs and pepper; mix until incorporated. The mixture should be moist but not pasty. If it seems too wet, add additional breadcrumbs.

4. Divide the stuffing into 4 equal parts; stuff the cavity of each trout. Wrap each fish individually in plastic wrap and refrigerate for at least 30 minutes. This step helps set the stuffing in the trout so it doesn't fall out when it cooks.

5. Preheat oven to 375°.

6. Season outside of trout with Cabernet Grill Cajun Seasoning. Place the cornmeal on a plate and roll the trout in the cornmeal, coating it evenly on all sides.

7. Heat a heavy skillet over medium heat and add oil. Sear trout on both sides until golden brown. Transfer the skillet to the oven.

8. Allow 10–15 minutes of cooking time, or until the flesh of the fish is opaque and flakes easily, and the stuffing is hot all the way through.

9. Heat a medium-sized sauté pan over medium heat; add the Toasted Pecan Brown Butter by golf ball-size spoonfuls. Allow the butter to sizzle and melt with the edges turning brown and fragrant. If the butter begins to burn, remove the pan from the heat. Allow butter to continue to melt and brown a bit, until about 80% has melted.

10. Remove the pan from the heat and pour butter over the trout. Serve immediately.

Toasted Pecan Brown Butter

Yield: About 1 cup

Ingredients:

½ cup toasted pecans, chopped
1½ sticks unsalted butter, room temperature
1 small shallot, minced
1 clove garlic, minced
2 teaspoons fresh lemon zest
1 tablespoon fresh chives, minced
½ teaspoon Tabasco Sauce
½ teaspoon kosher salt
Pinch freshly ground black pepper

Preparation:

1. Place all ingredients in a small bowl and stir with a rubber spatula until mixed together well.

2. Butter can be refrigerated for up to a week. Bring to room temperature before using.

Rosemary Cajun Bliss Potatoes

Serves 4–6

Ingredients:

1½ pounds Red Bliss potatoes (B size/small)
3 tablespoons unsalted butter, melted
2 teaspoons fresh rosemary, minced
3 cloves garlic, minced
1 tablespoon Cabernet Grill Cajun Seasoning
3 green onions, minced

Preparation:

1. Preheat oven to 400°.

2. Cut the potatoes into quarters and place in a large bowl.

3. Toss the potatoes with the butter, rosemary, garlic and Cabernet Grill Cajun Seasoning.

4. Pour onto a sheet pan and bake 45–50 minutes or until the potatoes are golden brown on the outside and fork-tender on the inside. Serve hot, topped with green onions.

ROSEMARY IN TEXAS

In many other parts of the country, rosemary is an expensive, exotic herb. Here in Texas, it's something we just step outside to harvest from the yard. It's a hardy, heat-tolerant evergreen that doesn't require much water and does double duty as a decorative landscape staple. All varieties are edible year 'round, and the purple flowers are a bonus when they bloom in spring.

ORANGE/VANILLA/CHILE BRINED DOUBLE CUT PORK CHOPS

with Sundried Strawberry Port Butter and Jalapeño Hoe Cakes | Serves 4

You're almost guaranteed a juicy chop when you cook double-cut pork chops correctly. For good measure, these are brined. The hints of vanilla and orange in the brine, and the way the meat is finished with Port butter, really take these pork chops to a higher level. Be sure you get double-cut, bone-in loin chops about 2 inches thick. The thickness makes a difference in the way the brine flavors and tenderizes the meat, and the way it cooks up juicy on the grill. Thinner chops may become mealy, tough and dry.

Ingredients:

4 pork loin chops, 10–12 ounces each, bone-in, double-cut
2 quarts Orange/Vanilla/Chile Brine (see recipe)
1 tablespoon cracked black pepper
1 cup Sundried Strawberry Port Butter (see recipe)
Jalapeño Hoe Cakes (see recipe)

Preparation:

1. Place pork chops in Orange/Vanilla/Chile Brine and refrigerate 3 hours.

2. Heat a mesquite grill to medium-high and sprinkle pork chops with black pepper. Press or pound the pepper into the meat with the heel of your hand.

3. Grill pork chops 8–9 minutes per side, or until the meat reaches medium on an instant-read thermometer inserted into the meat near the bone.

Orange/Vanilla/Chile Brine
Yield: 2 quarts

Ingredients:

1 quart water
⅔ cup kosher salt
½ cup granulated sugar
1 pasilla chile, toasted and crumbled
1 tablespoon Mexican vanilla extract
2 fresh Rio Grande Valley oranges, juiced
2 teaspoons fresh orange zest
3 cups ice water

Preparation:

1. Place 1 quart of water, salt and granulated sugar in a large saucepan and bring to a boil over high heat.

2. Remove pan from heat and add ice water, chile, vanilla, orange juice and zest.

3. Add ice water. This should cool the brine off enough so it can be used immediately. If the brine is any warmer than room temperature, place it in an ice bath or refrigerate it until it is cool enough to use.

Sundried Strawberry Port Butter
Yield: 1 cup

Ingredients:

3 ounces sundried strawberries
⅓ cup Texas Port wine
1 tablespoon safflower oil
1 shallot, minced
⅓ cup balsamic vinegar
1 cup Texas Port wine
⅓ cup granulated sugar
⅓ cup unsalted butter, cubed

Preparation:

1. Marinate strawberries in ⅓ cup of Port at room temperature for 30 minutes or until strawberries are softened.

2. Heat oil in a medium-sized saucepan over medium-low heat; add shallots, sweating them until they turn translucent. Do not brown the shallots.

3. Add balsamic vinegar, Port and sugar and increase heat to high. Reduce the liquid volume by two-thirds.

4. Remove saucepan from heat and whisk in cubes of butter until the butter has melted and the sauce has a velvety consistency.

5. Stir in softened strawberries and any remaining wine. Keep sauce warm and use as soon as possible.

Jalapeño Hoe Cakes

Yield: 12–16 cakes

These little corn cakes have just a touch of jalapeño for just the right bite. The contrast is delicious with the Sundried Strawberry Vanilla Pork Chops, but these also work great as an alternative to standard cornbread dressing for your holiday turkey.

Ingredients:

3 tablespoons granulated sugar
¾ cup all-purpose flour
1½ cups yellow cornmeal
3 teaspoons baking powder
1 teaspoon kosher salt
2 eggs
1¼ cups milk
¼ cup safflower oil
2 tablespoons fresh cilantro, minced
2 tablespoons green onions, minced
2 fresh jalapeños, minced
½ cup corn kernels, cooked
2 tablespoons red bell pepper, minced
¼ cup unsalted butter

Preparation:

1. Mix sugar, flour, cornmeal, baking powder and salt until well combined.

2. In a medium-sized mixing bowl, whip eggs together with milk until well blended. Stir in oil.

3. Add dry ingredients, cilantro, green onions, jalapeños, corn kernels and bell pepper to the egg mixture. Stir briefly until well combined, but do not over-mix.

4. Melt some of the butter in a large skillet over medium heat. Place spoonfuls of batter into the hot skillet to make small pancakes.

5. Cook until hoe cakes are golden brown and crispy on the edges, flipping only once. Continue making pancakes until all the batter is used. Serve hot.

DISH ASSEMBLY: *Place pork chops on a warm platter. Top with Sundried Strawberry Port Butter and serve beside Jalapeño Hoe Cakes.*

HOE CAKE HISTORY

Food historians believe these simple cornmeal pancakes originated within Native American cuisine. Over the years, field hands adapted the cornmeal-based recipe and cooked the pancakes on the flat surface of a hoe or shovel held over an open flame. The blade of the hoe essentially served as a griddle. Fortunately, these days we get to use a frying pan—without soil from the cornfield attached!

TASSO CHICKEN

with Crimini Mushrooms and Roasted Garlic Serrano Béarnaise
with Mesquite Grilled Okra | Serves 4

Chicken reflects other flavors well, and this dish proves
that point. The herb marinade starts the layering of flavors,
then it's grilled over fragrant wood and finished with a Cajun kick.

Ingredients:

2 pounds fresh chicken breast, boneless/skinless
4 cloves garlic, minced
2 tablespoons olive oil
¼ cup Sherry wine
½ teaspoon fresh thyme
Kosher salt and freshly ground black pepper
2 tablespoons safflower oil
2 cups crimini mushrooms, sliced
¾ cup Tasso ham, ⅓-inch dice
1 cup Roasted Garlic Serrano Béarnaise
　(see page 126)

Preparation:

1. Trim the chicken breast to remove any cartilage that may still be attached. Place chicken into a 1-gallon Ziploc bag.

2. Add garlic, olive oil, Sherry and thyme and carefully toss with the chicken. Seal the bag; refrigerate 12–24 hours (the longer the better), turning the bag every few hours to evenly marinate the chicken.

3. Heat a mesquite grill to medium-high and rub the cooking grates with a little oil to keep the chicken from sticking.

4. Cook the chicken for 4–5 minutes per side, until it is cooked through and the juices run clear when the meat is pierced with a knife. Do not overcook the chicken. Move the chicken to a warm platter to rest.

5. Add the safflower oil to a medium sauté pan on medium-high heat. Sauté mushrooms for about 3 minutes or until they soften and turn golden brown on the edges.

6. Add the Tasso ham and sauté 2 more minutes until the ham begins to caramelize a bit on the edges.

7. Spoon the mushroom/Tasso sauté over the chicken, then top with Roasted Garlic Serrano Béarnaise. Serve immediately.

Mesquite Grilled Okra | Serves 4–6

There's a Chef's Corner at the Fredericksburg Farmers Market where chefs like me get the privilege of working with two of the finest grill men in the area: Billy Ranck and Tommy Newman. They grill all day long and know more than most about how to cook vegetables on grills and smokers. I'm not often surprised by food, but Bill and Tommy taught this old dog a new trick, namely, that when you grill okra it removes the "slime" factor and produces a vegetable much like grilled asparagus. I love this recipe and now look forward to grilling okra every summer.

Ingredients:

1 pound young, small okra pods
2 tablespoons olive oil
2 teaspoons Cabernet Grill Cajun Seasoning

Preparation:

1. Heat a mesquite grill to medium-high heat.

2. Cut the okra in half lengthwise and toss in a bowl with olive oil and Cabernet Grill Cajun Seasoning.

3. Carefully place okra on the grill in a single layer and cook for 2–3 minutes per side or until it is a little blistered and charred. (Depending on how far apart your grill grates are, you may need to use a special vegetable grill pan.) Serve hot.

TASSO HAM

One of the tricks of Cajun cooking is the balance of saltiness and spice. Tasso is part of that balance. It's not really "ham" because it's usually made from pork shoulder, but it is cured like ham, with salt, sugar and hot spices. It's slow-smoked to a richness you can't find in any other product. Tasso isn't the kind of meat you'd eat in a sandwich; use little pieces of it when you want to add some kick to sauces, stews, soups and vegetables.

FREDERICKSBURG FARMERS MARKET

CHICKEN EGGS FOR SALE

½ doz. $3.00
1 doz. $5.00
2 doz. $9.00

Wander through your local farmers market and you'll gain a greater appreciation for the hard work and dedication of the families who provide your food. You'll see weathered faces smiling proudly about their goods, and busy hands that never stop working. Ask a vendor about their livelihood and you'll have a friend for life. The challenges of the weather in Texas—from drought to flood and from searing heat to hard freezes—are more than casual conversation at the Fredericksburg Farmers Market. Yet day after day these hardy folks work the land and care for livestock to bring us the freshest, best-tasting goods possible. I've been honored to be a guest chef at the FFM, where I create a dish entirely from market goods: local beef, lamb, chicken, fresh vegetables, herbs and lavender, sweet local fruits, farm-fresh cheeses and crusty breads. Our outdoor market is unique in that many of our area wineries also set up shop there—so we can all leave with fixings for a completely local meal.

The Texas Hill Country is home to all the ideal ingredients for a charmed ending to any meal: abundant fruits and nuts, fragrant lavender, lush vineyards. We take full advantage of these regional specialties, sending our guests home with sweet memories of a fine dinner. All of these recipes will be big hits with the dessert person in your life.

DESSERTS

★ ★ ★ ★ ★

★ ★ ★ ★ ★

Lavender is joining peaches as a well-known and hardy crop in the Texas Hill Country. Both come into season at the same time, and this recipe makes good use of both in a delicious fashion. I serve Alphonse Dotson's Gotas de Oro Muscat Canelli with this dessert — I think it's a match made in heaven!

Ingredients:

6 cups Fredericksburg peaches, peeled and sliced
1 tablespoon freshly-squeezed lemon juice
¼ cup local honey
¾ cup all-purpose flour
¾ cup rolled oats
¼ cup brown sugar, firmly packed
2 tablespoons lavender sugar*
½ teaspoon cinnamon
½ cup unsalted butter, softened
6 scoops vanilla bean ice cream

*CHEF'S NOTE: *You can find lavender sugar in many gourmet shops or online. To make your own, place ½ cup granulated sugar and 2 teaspoons of culinary lavender in a spice grinder or blender. Pulse until it has the consistency of powdered sugar.*

Preparation:

1. Preheat oven to 350°.

2. Spread peach slices in a 9-inch square pan.

3. Sprinkle with lemon juice, then drizzle with honey.

4. In medium bowl, mix together remaining ingredients using a pastry blender or fork.

5. Sprinkle dry mixture evenly over peaches.

6. Bake for 35–40 minutes or until top is golden brown.

7. Serve warm, topped with ice cream.

FREDERICKSBURG BLACKBERRY AND PECAN COBBLER
with Cinnamon Ice Cream | Serves 8

Native wild blackberries grow well in the Texas Hill Country soil, so our local fruit farmers have an easy time cultivating modern varieties with bigger, plumper berries. Blackberries and peaches are harvested at about the same time, so if you have peaches, make this a peach and pecan cobbler. Or, try mixing together a combination of both fruits for a full-on Fredericksburg treat.

Ingredients:

For blackberry filling:
5 cups Texas Hill Country blackberries, rinsed and well drained
½ cup unsalted butter
½ cup granulated sugar
2 teaspoons cinnamon
¼ teaspoon ground allspice
⅓ cup Texas Port wine
1 tablespoon cornstarch
1 tablespoon water
2 teaspoons Mexican vanilla extract

For cobbler batter:
½ cup unsalted butter, cubed
1 cup granulated sugar
1¼ cups all-purpose flour
1 teaspoon cinnamon
2 teaspoons baking powder
1 cup milk
½ cup pecan pieces, toasted

For serving:
8 scoops cinnamon ice cream

Preparation:

1. Preheat oven to 350°.

2. To prepare the filling: In a medium saucepan over medium heat, combine blackberries, butter, sugar, cinnamon, allspice and Port. Bring the mixture to a simmer.

3. Create a slurry by combining cornstarch and water in a small bowl. Stir slurry into berry mixture. Increase the heat, allowing the mixture to boil for 1 minute. The slurry will thicken the liquid and the mixture will become glossy. Reduce the heat to medium and cook for 3 minutes, stirring occasionally.

4. Remove from the heat, stir in vanilla, and allow mixture to cool.

5. To prepare the batter: Place butter in a 9x13 baking dish and set the dish in the preheated oven for 3–4 minutes until the butter melts.

6. Combine the remaining batter ingredients together in a bowl, mixing lightly until blended.

7. Pour batter into buttered baking dish. Cover batter with blackberry filling.

8. Bake at 350° for 30–45 minutes, or until golden brown and bubbly. Test for doneness by inserting a toothpick into an area of the cobbler that has no blackberry filling. If the toothpick comes out clean, the cobbler is done. If it comes out with batter attached to it, cook it a bit longer.

DISH ASSEMBLY: *Spoon warm cobbler into individual serving bowls and top with cinnamon ice cream.*

TEXAS HILLS VINEYARD SANGIOVESE SORBET

Yield: About 4 cups

You can omit the egg white if you choose, but adding it transforms the dessert from icy sorbet to creamier sherbet. For best results, use a good quality ice cream maker with a fast-action churn, which adds more air and lightness.

Ingredients:
1 750-liter bottle Texas Hills Vineyard
   Sangiovese
1 cup water
1½ cups granulated sugar
1 sprig fresh rosemary
½ lemon, zested and juiced
½ egg white, beaten

Preparation:

1. Place all ingredients, except the egg white, in a saucepan over high heat. Bring to a boil.

2. Reduce heat to low and simmer for 10 minutes.

3. Strain away rosemary and lemon zest. Allow mixture to cool completely.

4. Stir in egg white, if using, and pour mixture into an ice cream maker. Process according to manufacturer's directions.

5. Place in freezer overnight to set.

DEEP DISH KAHLÚA/WHITE CHOCOLATE CRÈME BRÛLÉE

Serves 4

I like the "crème" part of crème brûlée. This deep-dish style of the dessert is plenty creamy while still providing enough brûlée crunch. The white chocolate gives it additional body and extra richness.

Ingredients:

3 cups heavy cream
½ cup (3 ounces) white chocolate, chopped
3 tablespoons granulated sugar
⅓ cup Kahlúa liqueur
7 egg yolks
1 teaspoon Mexican vanilla extract
Additional granulated sugar

Preparation:

1. Preheat oven to 325°. Place an oven shelf in the middle position.

2. Pour cream into a small saucepan over medium heat. Bring just barely to a simmer and remove from the heat.

3. Add white chocolate and sugar to warmed cream, stirring until the sugar is dissolved and chocolate is melted. Set mixture aside to cool slightly.

4. Prepare a water bath: Place 4 8-ounce ovenproof ramekins in a roasting pan. Pour warm water into the roasting pan so it comes at least ¾ of the way up the sides of the ramekins. Be careful not to splash any water into the ramekins.

5. Whisk Kahlúa, egg yolks and vanilla into the cream mixture. Ladle mixture carefully into each ramekin, filling them nearly to the top.

6. Carefully place the roasting pan into the oven. Bake at 325° for about 1 hour. To check for doneness, gently tap the side of a ramekin with a spoon. The custard is properly set when the surface doesn't ripple from the tap. If the center is bubbling, it has been over-heated and you will need to start again.

7. Remove pan from oven and ramekins from water bath. Refrigerate overnight.

8. Prior to serving, top each ramekin with a thin layer of granulated sugar. To caramelize the sugar and create the brûlée, either place the ramekins under a pre-heated broiler, or use a kitchen torch. Sugar caramelizes quickly, so be careful that it doesn't burn.

9. Serve promptly.

RUBY RED GRAPEFRUIT BUTTERMILK PIE

with Polka Dot Sauce | Yield: 9-inch pie

Adding sweet Ruby Red Texas grapefruit takes this humble country pie to a new dimension. If you've never tried the Southern staple, this is a great place to start. If you grew up on it, this sure isn't your mama's buttermilk pie!

Ingredients:

1 9-inch pie crust
1 cup granulated sugar
3 eggs
3 tablespoons all-purpose flour
1½ cups buttermilk
¼ cup unsalted butter, melted
2 tablespoons freshly-squeezed Ruby Red
    grapefruit juice
1 tablespoon grated Ruby Red grapefruit zest
1 teaspoon Mexican vanilla extract
⅛ teaspoon freshly ground nutmeg

Preparation:

1. Preheat oven to 350°.

2. Use a fork to poke holes in the bottom of the pie crust, about ½-inch apart. Pre-bake the crust until light brown. The holes will prevent the dough from rising up and forming bubbles.

3. Beat eggs and sugar in a medium bowl until the mixture turns a light color and is fluffy.

4. Add the flour and mix lightly.

5. Add remaining ingredients and mix well.

6. Pour batter in pre-baked pie crust. Bake for 30 minutes, or until custard is set.

7. Allow pie to rest before serving at room temperature.

Polka Dot Sauce

Yield: 2 cups

Ingredients:

1½ cups freshly-squeezed Ruby Red
    grapefruit juice
1 tablespoon cornstarch
1 tablespoon water
⅓ cup granulated sugar
⅓ cup sour cream
2 tablespoons powdered sugar

Preparation:

1. Place grapefruit juice in a small saucepan and bring to a boil.

2. Stir the cornstarch and water together in a small bowl, making sure there are no lumps.

3. When the grapefruit juice is boiling, pour the cornstarch slurry into the liquid while whisking vigorously. Allow the mixture to boil for 2 minutes until it is slightly thickened and shiny.

4. Remove from the heat and set grapefruit sauce aside to cool.

5. Mix sour cream and powdered sugar in a small ramekin, using a spoon to create a smooth sauce.

6. Spoon the mixture into a small squeeze bottle, pastry bag with a fine tip, or use parchment paper to form a squeezable cone applicator.

DISH ASSEMBLY: *Ladle some of the grapefruit sauce on a white plate and roll the plate around so the sauce coats the plate in an even layer. Place a slice of pie in the center of the plate. Make white polka dots in the pink grapefruit sauce surrounding the pie, using the squeeze bottle or pastry bag*

BOURBON MANGO FLAMBÉ

with Mexican Vanilla Ice Cream and Chocolate Tortilla Stickers | Serves 4

The award-winning Mexican Vanilla Ice Cream I use in this recipe can be obtained from Clear River Pecan Bakery & Ice Cream Company in Fredericksburg. However, any good quality vanilla bean ice cream can be substituted.

Ingredients:

Peanut oil
¾ cup granulated sugar
1 teaspoon ground cinnamon
2 flour tortillas, cut in sixths
¼ cup white chocolate
¼ cup dark chocolate
½ stick unsalted butter
½ cup brown sugar
1 cinnamon stick
1 ounce Garrison Brothers Bourbon
¼ cup pineapple juice
1½ cups mango chunks, peeled
4 scoops Mexican Vanilla Ice Cream

Preparation:

For Tortilla Stickers:

1. Pour 3-inch depth of peanut oil in a fryer and heat to 350°.

2. Mix cinnamon and sugar together in a medium-sized bowl.

3. Fry tortilla triangles to a crispy golden color and toss immediately in a bowl with the cinnamon sugar. Shake off any excess sugar. Lay Tortilla Stickers on a sheet pan in a single layer.

4. Melt white and dark chocolates separately in a microwave, being careful to not overheat them.

5. Alternate drizzles of white and dark chocolate over Tortilla Stickers. Cool in refrigerator until chocolate sets. Set aside.

For Bourbon Mango Flambe:

1. Heat a sauté pan to medium-high heat. Add brown sugar, butter and cinnamon stick, stirring frequently.

2. When the mixture begins to bubble, add bourbon carefully, then ignite with a long-stem lighter. Shake the pan gently until the flames diminish. Add the pineapple juice carefully (it will bubble) and stir constantly to incorporate all ingredients.

3. Reduce the heat to low and add the mango chunks, stirring to warm them through.

DISH ASSEMBLY: *Place 1 scoop of ice cream into each of 4 bowls. Ladle hot mango flambé over ice cream and garnish by sticking 3 Tortilla Stickers upright into each ice cream scoop.*

GARRISON BROTHERS TEXAS STRAIGHT BOURBON

The Hill Country is filled with characters and independent spirit, and Garrison Brothers Distillery has a bit of both. The "first and oldest legal bourbon distillery in Texas" buys organic grain from Texas farmers—plus grows some of its own—and uses purified Hill Country rainwater as they hand-cook their bourbon mash. If you have a day free during your stay with us at the Cotton Gin Village, consider driving out east past Stonewall to tiny Hye for a tour of this fun, unique distillery in a "don't blink or you'll miss it" town. There are some great wineries along the way too— so you surely won't get thirsty.

GARRISON BROTHERS.
Distillery

GERMAN'S CHOCOLATE BREAD PUDDING

with Brandied Bing Cherry Ice Cream | Serves 6

In 1957, Dallas homemaker Mrs. George Clay, not a pastry chef from Germany, created the recipe for "German's Chocolate Cake," the dessert now referred to as "German Chocolate Cake." Her recipe called for German's Brand of baking chocolate—hence the name. We incorporate the same mix of German's chocolate, coconut and pecans into this bread pudding. It's as close as the Cabernet Grill comes to serving German food!

Ingredients:

3 cups day-old white bread, crusts removed
2 cups day-old brownies
2 ounces German's Brand Baking Chocolate, chopped
⅔ cup Coconut Pecan Frosting (see recipe)
3 whole eggs, lightly beaten
2 cups heavy cream
1 tablespoon Mexican vanilla extract
6 scoops Brandied Bing Cherry Ice Cream (see recipe)

Preparation:

1. Preheat oven to 350°.

2. Use a serrated bread knife to cut the bread and brownies into 1-inch cubes.

3. Divide the bread and brownies evenly between 6 8-ounce ceramic ramekins.

4. Divide the chopped chocolate and Coconut Pecan Frosting evenly between the ramekins.

5. In a medium bowl, whisk the eggs, cream and vanilla together until well blended.

6. Pour the cream mixture evenly into each of the ramekins and use a small spoon to push the bread mixture down and around a bit, so that the cream covers the bread, and the chocolate and frosting are somewhat distributed through the mixture.

7. Bake on a cookie sheet for about 45 minutes or until the tops are golden brown and the custard mixture has set.

Coconut Pecan Frosting

Yield: 2+ cups

Ingredients:

½ cup granulated sugar
½ cup evaporated milk
2 tablespoons unsalted butter
1 whole egg
1 egg yolk
⅔ cup sweetened flake coconut
½ cup San Saba pecans, toasted and chopped
½ teaspoon Mexican vanilla extract

Preparation:

1. Place the sugar, milk, butter and eggs in a small saucepan over medium heat. Cook, stirring constantly, until the mixture starts to bubble.

2. Remove from the heat and stir in the coconut, pecans and vanilla.

3. Allow to cool fully before using.

Brandied Bing Cherry Ice Cream
Yield: 1½ quarts

Ingredients:
¾ cup Bing cherries, pitted and cut into quarters
¼ cup Presidente Brandy
4 cups half and half
6 egg yolks
1 teaspoon Mexican vanilla extract
1¼ cups granulated sugar

Preparation:

1. Place cherries and brandy in a small bowl and stir. Marinate overnight in the refrigerator, stirring a few times when possible.

2. Mix cream and egg yolks, and cook in a double boiler over medium-high heat until mixture starts to thicken slightly, stirring constantly. To test for when to remove it from the heat, dip a wooden spoon into the mixture. When you can draw a line through the cream coating the spoon, remove it from the heat. Add the vanilla and sugar while the cream is still hot, stirring to dissolve.

3. Allow mixture to cool completely.

4. Pour mixture into an ice cream maker and follow manufacturer's instructions. When the ice cream begins to set, fold in the refrigerated cherries and their juice.

CHEF'S NOTE: *Due to the alcohol content of the marinated cherries, the ice cream may not set up firmly in the ice cream maker. For a more solid ice cream, just place it in the freezer for a few hours prior to serving.*

DISH ASSEMBLY: *Top each ramekin of warm bread pudding with a scoop of Brandied Bing Cherry Ice Cream.*

BOOZY BERRY LAVENDER SHORTCAKE
with Vanilla Orange Pastry Cream | Serves 8

Texture and taste are at the center of this popular Cabernet Grill dessert that features two Hill Country flavors—berries and lavender. It's a little showy too, so you're sure to get rave reviews every time you treat your guests to it.

Boozy Berry Lavender Shortcake with Vanilla Orange Pastry Cream
Serves 8

Ingredients:
8 Lavender Shortcake Biscuits (see recipe)
3 cups Boozy Berries (see recipe)
2 cups Vanilla Orange Pastry Cream (see recipe)
1 cup fresh sweetened whipped cream
Powdered sugar

Lavender Shortcake Biscuits
Yield: 8 biscuits

Ingredients:
1 tablespoon granulated sugar
1 teaspoon dried lavender
½ cup granulated sugar
3 cups all-purpose flour
1 tablespoon baking powder
½ teaspoon baking soda
¾ teaspoon kosher salt
1½ sticks unsalted butter, chilled
½ cup heavy cream
2 large eggs

Preparation:
1. Preheat oven to 375°.

2. Make lavender sugar by placing 1 tablespoon sugar and the lavender into an electric coffee grinder. Pulse until it has the consistency of powdered sugar.

3. Sift the lavender sugar, the other ½ cup sugar, flour, baking powder, baking soda and salt into the bowl of a food processor.

4. Cut the butter into ¼-inch slices and add to food processor.

5. Pulse the flour/butter mixture until it becomes coarse, with pea-size pieces of butter throughout. Place this dry mixture into a medium-sized bowl and make a well in the center.

6. In a separate bowl, use a fork to beat together the cream and eggs until thoroughly combined. Pour the mixture into the flour/butter well.

7. Fold the dry mix into the wet mix, just until large clumps start to form.

8. Turn the mixture out onto a work surface and knead it with your hands until it just begins to come together, no more than about 30 seconds. Do not overwork the dough or the biscuits will be tough.

9. Form the dough into a log about 8 inches long and 3 inches wide.

10. Slice the dough into 8 equal disks. Place the disks on a parchment paper-lined baking tray, about 2 inches apart from each other.

11. Bake at 375° for 15–20 minutes or until golden brown.

Boozy Berries
Yield: 3 cups

Ingredients:
3 cups ripe strawberries, trimmed and sliced
⅓ cup powdered sugar, sifted
2 tablespoons Grand Marnier

Preparation:
1. Place all ingredients in a medium-sized bowl.

2. Toss together well and allow to marinate for at least 30 minutes before serving.

Vanilla Orange Pastry Cream
Yield: About 2½ cups

Ingredients:
1 vanilla bean
2 cups milk
½ cup granulated sugar
1 whole egg
2 egg yolks
¼ cup cornstarch
2 tablespoons unsalted butter
2 teaspoons grated orange zest

Preparation:
1. Split the vanilla bean lengthwise and, using a paring knife, scrape the seeds from the inside of the bean into a small bowl. Set aside.

2. Place the vanilla bean pod, milk and sugar into a medium-sized heavy-bottomed saucepan, and bring the mixture to a boil over medium-high heat. Remove and discard the vanilla bean pod from the milk, leaving the milk on the heat.

3. Place the egg, egg yolk and cornstarch in a medium bowl and whisk until smooth. Slowly ladle a thin stream of boiling milk into the egg mixture, tempering it until the milk has been incorporated. Pour the egg/milk mixture back into the saucepan and slowly return it to a boil, stirring constantly with a rubber spatula so that the mixture does not burn or scorch.

4. Once the mixture begins to boil and thicken, reduce the heat to medium and cook for 2 minutes stirring constantly.

5. Remove from the heat. Stir in the butter, reserved vanilla bean seeds and orange zest.

6. Pour warm cream into a small glass casserole or pie dish. Cover with plastic wrap pressed directly onto the surface of the pastry cream so it doesn't develop a skin.

7. Refrigerate until completely cool before using. This mixture can be refrigerated for about 5 days.

DISH ASSEMBLY: *For each serving, carefully split a Lavender Shortcake Biscuit in half, using a serrated knife and a very gentle sawing motion. Place the bottom half of the shortcake in the center of the plate and top with about ½ cup of Vanilla Orange Pastry Cream. Top the pastry cream with some of the Boozy Berries and a dollop of whipped cream. Top with the other half of the biscuit, forming a sandwich. Drizzle some of the berry juice on top of the biscuit. Place some powdered sugar in a small sieve (or fine mesh colander) and shake a little sugar on top of the shortcake and the plate as garnish. Serve immediately.*

FREDERICKSBURG STRAWBERRIES

In April and May, you can get fresh strawberries straight from the fields within a 5 minute drive of the Cotton Gin Village. Itz Garden, Engel Farms and Marburger Orchard, to name a few, represent the generations of Hill Country family farmers who understand how to coax sweetness from the earth. You can even pick your own at many places, including Marburger Orchard, or visit their farm stand for a variety of just-harvested fruits and veggies. Family farms and fresh produce are what make cooking and dining in the Hill Country so special.

CHICKEN FRIED PECAN PIE

with Chocolate Jack Daniel's Ice Cream | Serves 8

A crunchy coating makes all the difference in this slightly over-the-top dessert. Will Texans chicken-fry anything? Maybe. But this works particularly well and is a repeat favorite for a lot of our guests.

Ingredients:

1 Texas Pecan Pie, partially frozen (see recipe)
1 cup all-purpose flour
2 cups milk
1 egg, beaten
2 cups Panko breadcrumbs
8 scoops Chocolate Jack Daniel's Ice Cream
    (see recipe)
Peanut oil

Preparation:

1. Fill a deep fryer with peanut oil, according to manufacturer's directions, and heat to 350°.

2. Create a breading station with 3 bowls. Place flour in the first bowl, a mixture of the milk and egg in the second, and Panko in the third.

3. Cut partially frozen pecan pie into 8 slices. Dredge each slice in flour to coat completely. Shake off any excess flour. Next, dip the pie slice into the egg mixture, coating completely, then coat with Panko breadcrumbs. Follow these steps with each slice of pie.

4. Place 1 or 2 pie slices at a time into hot oil and cook for about 3 minutes, until golden brown and warm in the center. Keep pie slices warm as you continue to cook all the remaining slices.

Texas Pecan Pie
Yield: 9-inch pie

Ingredients:

1¼ cups San Saba pecan pieces
3 eggs
1 cup dark corn syrup
½ cup granulated sugar
⅓ cup unsalted butter, melted
1 tablespoon Mexican vanilla
⅛ teaspoon kosher salt
1 9-inch pie crust

Preparation:

1. Preheat oven to 350°.

2. Spread pecan pieces on a cookie sheet and toast in oven for 3 minutes.

3. Beat eggs well in a medium size bowl. Stir in corn syrup, sugar, butter, vanilla and salt.

4. Fold in toasted pecans. Pour mixture into the pie crust.

5. Bake at 350° for about 50 minutes or until a knife inserted halfway between the center and edge of the pie comes out clean.

6. Allow pie to cool before slicing.

Chocolate Jack Daniel's Ice Cream
Yield: 1½ quarts

Ingredients:
4 cups half and half
6 egg yolks
1 cup granulated sugar
4 ounces dark chocolate, chopped
¼ cup Jack Daniel's Whiskey

Preparation:

1. Mix cream and egg yolks and cook in a double boiler until mixture starts to thicken slightly, stirring continually. To test for when to remove it from the heat, dip a wooden spoon into the mixture. When you can draw a line through the cream coating the spoon, remove it from the heat.

2. Add the sugar, chocolate and whiskey while the cream is still hot, stirring to dissolve the sugar and melt the chocolate.

3. Allow mixture to cool completely.

4. Pour mixture into an ice cream maker and follow manufacturer's instructions.

CHEF'S NOTE: *Due to the alcohol content of the whiskey, the ice cream may not set up firmly in the ice cream maker. For a more solid ice cream, just place it in the freezer for a few hours prior to serving.*

DISH ASSEMBLY: *Top each slice of Chicken Fried Pecan Pie with a scoop of Chocolate Jack Daniel's Ice Cream.*

CLEAR RIVER PECAN COMPANY ICE CREAM

We serve a lot of ice cream at the Cabernet Grill, so we rely on the expert confectioners right down the road to make the very best. The Clear River Pecan Company churns 50 or so ice cream flavors in its old-timey sweet shop on Main Street, making it a must-do stop for kids of every age. They make a few special adult flavors just for us, including Chocolate Jack Daniel's and Brandied Bing Cherry. As you stroll downtown, stop in for a free sample and a trip down memory lane, knowing you probably won't leave without a sack full of handmade candies loaded with local pecans.

SALT & PEPPER CHOCOLATE PANNA COTTA

with Ported Sundried Strawberries | Serves 6

I'm crazy about the caramel undertones and berry flavors in Torre di Pietra Tango Port. I developed this recipe to pair with it for a wine tasting event and it was a perfect match. The hint of black pepper makes the berries pop with flavor, and brings out the berry in the wine. The panna cotta is delicious, but truth be told, I'd be happy with just a glass of this Port for dessert.

Ingredients:

1 envelope unflavored gelatin
2 tablespoons cold water
2 cups heavy cream
¾ cup half and half
½ cup caramel ice cream topping, jarred
4 ounces bittersweet dark chocolate, chopped
¼ cup Torre di Pietra Tango Port
1 teaspoon flaky sea salt
½ cup Ported Sundried Strawberries (see recipe)
Freshly ground black pepper

Preparation:

1. Place the water and gelatin in a small bowl and let it stand for 10 minutes to soften.

2. In a saucepan over medium-high heat, combine heavy cream and half and half. Bring to a boil, then remove from heat immediately.

3. While still hot, stir in caramel topping and chopped chocolate, mixing well until melted and fully incorporated.

4. Add softened gelatin and stir to dissolve completely.

5. Add Port and sea salt. Stir to incorporate.

6. Divide mixture evenly between 6 large martini glasses. Cover and place in refrigerator for at least 4 hours or until firmly set.

Ported Sundried Strawberries

Yield: ½ cup

Ingredients

½ cup sundried strawberries
¼ cup Torre di Pietra Tango Port

Preparation:

1. Combine berries and Port in a small bowl.

2. Allow to marinate for 2 hours at room temperature before serving.

DISH ASSEMBLY: *Just before serving, grind a little black pepper on the surface of the panna cotta. Top with a few Ported Sundried Strawberries.*

PAIR IT WITH PORT

As a general rule, dessert wines should be sweeter than the dessert itself. That's why a glass of Port pairs well with this Panna Cotta. And since you have the bottle open to use in the recipe, why not enjoy it?

TEXAS HILL COUNTRY WINERIES

The dozen or so wineries on Wine Road 290—from west of Fredericksburg to east of Johnson City—are just the tip of the iceberg of the vast number of the state's wineries—273 at last count. There are about 50 wineries and more than 25 vineyards in the Texas Hill Country alone and that number grows every year. In fact, The Texas Hill Country is second only to Napa, California as the fastest growing wine region in the United States. It's no wonder. The Texas Hill Country is a more affordable destination and not nearly as crowded as Napa. It's in the middle of the country and easy to reach from almost anywhere. It's also in the center of the state, drawing visitors from Houston, Dallas, Austin and San Antonio. What's more, the views are similar to the vistas you'd see in Sonoma, Napa and Pasa Robles, with rolling hills and wineries atop scenic bluffs. Factor in the warm Southern hospitality at the tasting rooms, restaurants and inns, and it's clear why the Texas Wine Country has an ever-increasing fan base.

So when is the best time to visit? Whenever you're here. Everything is in bloom in spring, the busiest and most colorful vineyard touring season. Roadsides and fields lined with wildflowers lay a carpet of welcome to the vines as they bud break and fill out. Winemakers offer tastes of their favorites from the past and ponder the future vintage possibilities. As summer winds down the vines are heavy with fruit. That's when harvest begins and the aroma of ripe grapes hangs in the air. Take a turn stomping grapes during a celebration of the fermentation gods. Then again, many people love visiting Texas Hill Country wineries during fall and winter, when the air is cooler and the passionate winemakers have time to talk at length about their craft. Some visitors never go to a vineyard at all, and simply settle into one of the many area tasting rooms to fill their days and nights with flights of Texas wines.

When you stay at the Cotton Gin Village, dozens of wines from across the state are just a short stroll away. The Cabernet Grill features the largest Texas wine list of any restaurant in the state, putting award-winners and up-and-comers easily within your reach. Our staff will help you pair any dish with an ideal wine by the glass or bottle. And of course, you can always take those unfinished bottles back to your cabin to enjoy later.

THE STATE OF HILL COUNTRY WINE

The Texas Hill Country was named "One of the Top 10 Wine Travel Destinations in the World for 2014" by Wine Enthusiast Magazine.

60
Wineries in the Texas Hill Country Region

450
Acres Planted in the Texas Hill Country

Fredericksburg ★

The Texas Hill Country

300
Vineyards in Texas

The Texas Hill Country Wine Appellation

Credit Susan and Ed Auler of Fall Creek Vineyards for legally formalizing the official Texas Hill Country wine appellation in 1991, now the 2nd largest AVA in the United States. Fall Creek Vineyards, established in 1975 in Tow, Texas, is one of the Hill Country's oldest and most scenic vineyards, and the Aulers are beloved icons of Texas wines. Meritus, their super-premium red wine, is hailed by experts, winning awards with every release. It's certainly at the top of *my* personal list of best Texas Hill Country wines.

Stats are approximate. Sources: Texas Hill Country Wineries Association, Texas Wine and Grape Growers Association, Texas A&M University

Some people might consider wine an "extra" ingredient:
We consider it an essential elixir of life. In that vein,
you'll find recipes in this section that are vital elements
in our Cabernet Grill dishes, as well as a couple
of salsas we just can't live without.

EXTRAS

★ ★ ★ ★ ★

★ ★ ★ ★ ★

CABERNET GRILL CAJUN SEASONING
Yield: 1½ cups

Think of this as salt and pepper with a bang (not a bam)! This all-purpose seasoning is listed as an ingredient in many of my recipes, so make plenty and keep it on hand. Sprinkle it on hot popcorn, pita chips fresh from the oven, roasted or steamed vegetables, roasted nuts, grilled chicken, in soups ... the possibilities are endless. When you visit the Cotton Gin Village, you can always pick up a few jars in our store too, and bring a taste of Fredericksburg home for friends. Or order it online from us and we'll send as much as you want right to your door.

Ingredients:

4 tablespoons paprika
3 tablespoons table salt
2 tablespoons granulated garlic
2 tablespoons dried oregano
2 tablespoons dried basil
2 tablespoons onion powder
1 tablespoon dried thyme
1 tablespoon freshly ground black pepper
1 tablespoon ground white pepper
1 tablespoon cayenne pepper

Preparation:

1. Place all ingredients in a bowl and mix well.

2. Store in an airtight container.

CABERNET GRILL DRY RUB | Yield: 1 cup

Used in my recipe for Dry Rubbed Certified Angus Beef Tenderloin Tails. Makes enough to season any cut of beef, pork or chicken you throw on the grill. It's great on shrimp and fish, too!

Ingredients:

2 tablespoons kosher salt
4 tablespoons brown sugar
1 tablespoon ground cumin
1 tablespoon granulated garlic
2 tablespoons freshly ground black pepper
4 tablespoons paprika
2 tablespoons chili powder

Preparation:

1. Place all ingredients in a bowl and mix well.

2. Store in an airtight container.

BUG JUICE SALSA | Yield: 3 cups

We like coming up with fun names for this bright green salsa—Soylent Green Salsa, Windshield Wiper Salsa—when we sell it at the Fredericksburg Farmers Market. It doesn't seem to matter what we call it, we always sell out.

Ingredients:

3 cups fresh tomatillos, husked
3 serrano chiles, stems removed
2 cloves garlic
½ bunch fresh cilantro leaves
2 500 mg Vitamin C tablets
½ cup water
Kosher salt and freshly ground black pepper

Preparation:

1. Place all ingredients in a food processor and puree.

2. Taste and adjust seasoning with salt and pepper.

3. Keep refrigerated.

The Secret Ingredient

Don't worry. The Vitamin C tabs won't change the taste of the salsa. What they will do is keep it bright green longer. Vitamin C, or ascorbic acid, is a water-soluble vitamin that serves as "secret ingredient" in keeping many prepared foods looking great and tasting fresh longer. It's a bonus that it's really good for you too.

SPICY TOASTED PEPITAS | Yield: 1 cup

Ingredients:

1 cup pepitas (pumpkin seeds), raw, hulled
1 tablespoon unsalted butter, melted
½ teaspoon Cabernet Grill Cajun Seasoning

Preparation:

1. Preheat oven to 350°.

2. In a small bowl, stir pepitas with butter and seasoning until evenly coated.

3. Line a cookie sheet with parchment paper. Spread pepitas in a single layer.

4. Bake for 12 minutes, until fragrant and toasted.

5. Allow to cool. Store in a well-sealed container and use within a week.

Ingredients:

1 tablespoon safflower oil
3 pasilla chiles
6 chiles de arbol
2 ancho chiles
2 small tomatoes, cores removed
2 serrano chiles, stems removed
¼ small onion, peeled
2 cloves garlic
1 teaspoon ground cumin
¾ cup chicken stock
Kosher salt and freshly ground black pepper

Preparation:

1. Prepare a grill to medium-high heat and brush the grates with a little oil to keep the food from sticking.

2. Lightly toast the dried chiles on the grill until fragrant. Remove to a small bowl and cover chiles in boiling water. Allow the chiles to steep and soften for about 10 minutes. Drain the water and allow the chiles to cool enough for you to handle them.

3. Roast the tomatoes, Serrano chiles, onion and garlic on the grill until they're charred and blistered on all sides. Move vegetables to the bowl of a food processor.

4. Remove the stems from the dried chiles; slit them open and remove and discard the seeds.

5. Add the dried chiles to the roasted vegetables in the food processor. Add cumin and chicken stock, and puree the mixture.

6. Adjust seasoning with salt and pepper.

DEVELOPING DEEPER FLAVORS

It takes very little time to make the most of common ingredients like cumin. Rather than buying ground cumin, which loses much of its flavor during processing, buy whole cumin seeds. Lightly toast them in a dry skillet over medium heat until you begin to smell the aroma rising from the seeds. Let them cool, then grind them in a mortar and pestle or electric spice grinder. It takes just minutes, but makes a big difference in the flavor of the dish.

BURTWELL FAMILY TABLE MUSTARD
Yield: A tiny bit

When I was growing up, any time my mother made a roast for dinner she also made this condiment. Whenever I use it now, it brings back fond memories of the funny faces we would make as kids when this potent mustard hit our palate. Don't be fooled: This simple little recipe packs a big punch, so serve it sparingly.

Ingredients:
1 tablespoon Colman's English Mustard Powder
2 teaspoons water

Preparation:
1. Mix ingredients in a shot glass and let the mixture rest for 20 minutes before serving.

CHEF'S NOTE: *The mustard loses its potency after a few hours, so discard what you don't use as an accompaniment to hot roasted meats.*

CABERNET GRILL WASABI STEAK SAUCE
Yield: A little more than 1 cup

In the years that I have operated the Cabernet Grill, we have never allowed a bottle of commercial steak sauce to be placed on any of the tables in my restaurant. I simply refuse to let our guests ruin a great steak. Our kitchen prepares several delicious accompaniments for our steaks, and this one simply puts any store-bought sauce to shame.

Ingredients:
2 tablespoons balsamic vinegar
1 tablespoon wasabi powder
¼ cup Worcestershire sauce
¼ cup Dijon mustard
¼ cup molasses
¼ cup Original Louisiana Hot Sauce

Preparation:
1. Mix balsamic vinegar and wasabi powder together until smooth.

2. Whisk in the remaining ingredients.

CHEF'S NOTE: *Best served within a few days for maximum punch; will keep in the refrigerator for up to a month.*

CABERNET GRILL DRY RUBS

CAPER GREEN OLIVE STEAK SAUCE

Yield: 1 cup

This is a loose interpretation of the classic Argentine chimichurri sauce that is served throughout South America as an accompaniment to grilled meats. The vinegary capers and peppery Tabasco really complement the robust, earthy flavors imparted by the grill. It's more than a steak sauce; try it as a quick fish marinade too.

Ingredients:

½ bunch fresh parsley, minced
¼ cup pitted green olives, minced
2 tablespoons capers, rinsed
½ cup extra virgin olive oil
2 cloves garlic, minced
½ shallot, minced
1 teaspoon Tabasco Sauce
½ teaspoon freshly ground black pepper

Preparation:

1. Mix all ingredients together. Allow flavors to meld for at least an hour at room temperature before serving.

GREEN PEPPERCORN HORSERADISH CREAM SAUCE

Yield: 1 cup

Most often this sauce is served with prime rib, yet it works equally as well with grilled steaks and chops. The green peppercorns give it a little extra zing—something we love in the Texas Hill Country.

Ingredients:

¼ cup prepared horseradish
¼ cup sour cream
¼ cup mayonnaise
1 tablespoon green peppercorns in brine, rinsed
½ teaspoon freshly ground black pepper
Pinch kosher salt

Preparation:

1. Stir all ingredients together.

CHEF'S NOTE: *Best served right away for maximum punch; will keep in the refrigerator for a day or two. Stir well before serving.*

COTTON GIN VILLAGE
BREAKFAST GRANOLA

Cotton Gin Village Granola is a sweet way to greet the morning, whether you're waking up in the Texas Hill Country or your own home. It's loaded with rolled oats, cornflakes, coconut, nuts and seeds, baked in a spiced brown sugar and honey coating, then mixed with a generous amount of dried fruits. It's so good that I'm asked for this recipe more than I'm asked for any other recipe. I've been told it's addictively delicious and a sweet reminder of a relaxing visit to our Hill Country spot. Rather than include the recipe in this book, we've included a link to it from the home page of our website, CottonGinVillage.com. Be sure to make enough to give as gifts!

INDEX OF RECIPES